Dear Reader:

The book you are about to read is the latest bestseller from St. Martin's True Crime Library, the imprint that has been called "the leader in true crime!" Each month we offer you a fascinating account of the latest, most sensational crimes that have captured the national attention. St. Martin's is the publisher of bestselling author VANISHED AT SEA, the story of a con man who posed as a yacht buyer in order to lure his victims out to sea, then robbed them and threw them overboard to their deaths. John Glatt's riveting and horrifying SECRETS IN THE CELLAR shines a light on the man who shocked the world when it was revealed that he had kept his daughter locked in his hidden basement for 24 years. In the Edgar-nominated WRITTEN IN BLOOD, Diane Fanning looks at Michael Petersen, a Marine-turned-novelist found guilty of beating his wife to death and pushing her down the stairs of their home—only to reveal another similar death from his past. In the book you now hold, WHEN EVIL RULES, bestselling author Michele R. McPhee takes a look at the crimes of a Cape Cod town—and the man who may have been responsible.

St. Martin's True Crime Library gives you the stories behind the headlines. Our authors take you right to the scene of the crime and into the minds of the most notorious murderers to show you what really makes them tick. St. Martin's True Crime Library paperbacks are better than the most terrifying thriller, because it's all true! The next time you want a crackling good read, make sure it's got the St. Martin's True Crime Library logo on the spine—you'll be up all night!

Charles E. Spicer, Jr.
Executive Editor, St. Martin's True Crime Library

TITLES BY
MICHELE R. MCPHEE

Heartless

When Evil Rules

FROM THE TRUE CRIME LIBRARY OF
ST. MARTIN'S PAPERBACKS

WHEN
EVIL
RULES

Michele R. McPhee

St. Martin's Paperbacks

WHEN EVIL RULES

Copyright © 2009 by Michele R. McPhee.

Cover photo of man's eye by Michael Bader / Jupiter Images. Cover photo of lighthouse by Jupiter Images..

For information address St. Martin's Press, 175 Fifth Avenue, New York, NY 10010.

ISBN: 0-312-94775-5
EAN: 978-0-312-94775-0

Printed in the United States of America

St. Martin's Paperbacks edition / August 2009

St. Martin's Paperbacks are published by St. Martin's Press, 175 Fifth Avenue, New York, NY 10010.

10 9 8 7 6 5 4 3 2 1

*This book is dedicated to all
who crusade against corruption.*

ACKNOWLEDGMENTS

This book would have been impossible without help from the crusaders against corruption, including retired Falmouth Police Officer Richard Smith. Others operate with anonymity, and they know who they are.

I would also like to thank Allison Caplin and Charlie Spicer at St. Martin's Paperbacks—the best editors in the business—for the time spent on this manuscript. Of course my dogged literary agent Jane Dystel deserves endless kudos for her patience and direction. I'd also like to thank George Tobia, the extraordinarily talented lawyer who braves the Boston winters but is the talk of the town in Hollywood.

I want to give a nod to my colleagues at 96.9 FM WTKK, Boston's Talk Evolution, where I have a nightly radio show. They have been enormously supportive and generous with time. A special thanks to program director Grace Blazer.

Falmouth is a small town and distrustful of outsiders. Without Craig Galvin's hospitality, I would not have been able to make the necessary connections in Falmouth to forge forward. And without the lemon-poppy pancakes at the Moonakis eatery, who would have the stamina to write all summer long in a gorgeous beach town like Falmouth? Thank you to Paul Rifkin, the owner of the best breakfast joint on Cape Cod, and his great staff, especially Karen. I also want to acknowledge the bravery of Loretta Gilfoy in her fight for justice.

INTRODUCTION

I have been a crime reporter for two decades—working as a police bureau chief at two major city newspapers, the *New York Daily News* and the *Boston Herald*. My shoe-leather reporting across the country has netted me a variety of police sources, and the time spent in courtrooms has helped me navigate even the most difficult clerks' offices.

It was interviews with law enforcement sources and hours spent culling over piles and piles of court documents that gave me the information that I needed to write this book. But I must point out that while Melvin Reine is certainly a suspect in a frighteningly long list of crimes, he has not been charged or convicted of the three homicides law enforcement officials believe he was involved in. Reine is currently in extremely critical condition at a psychiatric hospital for the criminally insane in Massachusetts, so even if police and prosecutors could build a case, it is unlikely that he will ever be sane enough to face a trial.

Michele R. McPhee
February, 2009

WHEN
EVIL
RULES

ONE

The early morning light that comes with sunrise on Cape Cod is often breathtaking, as it was on May 10, 2005, when Michael Domingues showed up at 657 East Falmouth Highway. His early arrival served two purposes: he worked for Shirley Reine at her lucrative trash-hauling company, and he was her lover.

While Domingues was a small man who stood just five-foot-three, he was ruggedly built. He was not a handsome man, but he had a fierceness that women found attractive. Certainly Shirley Reine did.

Domingues noted the crimson haze over the cranberry bog across the street from Shirley's house, and out of habit he scanned the windows of the four houses that ringed the tight cluster of cottages that made up the Reine compound to make sure no one was looking out the window. The homes abutted one another in the shape of a horseshoe, and were upscale versions of the classic Cape Cod saltbox with cedar shingles weathered gray by the salty air and harsh New England winters. Each house was ringed by a cedar-post fence and had impeccably manicured lawns and landscaped flowers.

The Reine compound was a massive one—the family's property stretched to the marshes that abutted the land, and went back at least a mile into a wooded area. That's where the Reines kept the heavy equipment and warehouse that made up the family business, Five Star Enterprises, a garbage removal company that pulled in roughly $5 million a year in profits. The compound was marked with a granite boulder that Melvin had branded with an etching of the family name underneath a truck symbolizing the hauling business.

But no one who grew up in Falmouth or spent any substantial amount of time there needed the reminder. Everyone in town knew who Melvin Reine Sr. was and where he lived. Most locals stayed clear of the area and would not even pull a U-turn in the Reines' circular driveway for fear of attracting the old man's ire. Some would glance up at the gilded fox on top of the patriarch's roof—a taunt of sorts to the town from Melvin Reine, who would often brag that he was as sinister and crafty as a fox—and think about how the town cops often turned a blind eye to his well-known arson threats. If you crossed him, he would throw a spent match. When that happened, something was going to burn. And Melvin Reine would never be implicated.

But things had been quiet since 2001, when Melvin Reine could not escape being charged with assault and battery for allegedly attacking a tourist in a parking lot and threatening her with a baseball bat. Even his closest friends on the Falmouth police force could not make a violent wrongdoing like that go away. He was declared legally insane and sent to an insane asylum—a decision made after a psychiatric professional interviewed him under a judge's order and found that Melvin Reine was anything but lucid. He spoke of hallucinations and had a grandiosity that was concerning, especially to those in the Cape Cod judicial system who had become well-acquainted with Reine and the madman's forty-year reign of terror over the small town he'd grown up in. He was what those who work in the court system call a "frequent flyer"—a man who had faced a Cape Cod judge more than a dozen times since he was old enough to be charged as an adult.

Shirley had been running Five Star Enterprises since. Domingues had taken on the bulk of the heavy lifting that kept the company running, while Shirley handled the business end and dealt with the customers on her trash route. Over the years, Shirley purportedly came to rely on Domingues for more than his business acumen, and rumors began to circulate that she was relying on him for his bedroom prowess as well. In order to spend time together, Domingues, a married man, would come to work around 5:30 a.m. with two cups of Dunkin' Donuts coffee lightened by cream and sweeter than most would have it. (New Englanders called the brew a large regular.) If the day was slow, they could sip coffee at Shirley's kitchen table and watch the sunrise over the cranberry bog across the street from her house. On that spectacular May New England morning, Domingues looked up, noted the purple, cloudless sky and smiled to himself. *It's going to be a good day.*

That feeling of ease would be short-lived. Domingues rang the doorbell at Shirley's house after setting one of the Styrofoam coffee cups on a railing. Shirley did not answer. He could hear her five dachshund dogs barking in the background, unusual frantic yelps that he had not heard from them before. Shirley's beloved pet goat Ricky bleated out back.

He pressed the pad of his index finger hard against the bell and listened as the chimes rang throughout the house. He tried calling Shirley on her cell, on her home phone and on the business line. No answer. Then he strode to the attached garage to see if her car was there. He hoisted himself onto his tiptoes, peered through the small square windows of the garage and spotted Shirley's long, slender legs unmoving on the cement ground. Her jeans were splattered with red. He began to scream, "Those motherfuckers!" The curses came over and over like a mantra.

He ran up the stairs to an office above the garage. It was locked. He began to drive his legs into the door. With each ferocious kick he delivered to the garage door, he screamed, "Those motherfuckers!" After what seemed like hours, the door was finally forced from its hinges. Woken by the commotion, an extended member of the Reine family called 911 from one of the houses on the compound.

For hours before Domingues arrived, Shirley Reine's body had lain splayed in the same spot, undiscovered. A gunman had pumped two shots into her at point-blank range.

The first bullet smashed into Shirley Reine's chest as she'd climbed out of her green Nissan Maxima. It knocked her to the concrete floor of her garage, where the bloodstain on her yellow blouse blossomed into the shape and color of a pomegranate. The second pierced the right side of her head.

When Domingues finally smashed his way into the garage, he noted Shirley's back was slumped against the driver's-side door, her head on the floor next to the gas and brake pedals. Her curly black hair was sticky with congealed blood. Her petite hands were spread out as if she'd tried to break her fall when the bullets hit. Investigators would later discover that when the gun blasts had killed her, Reine was still digesting the dinner she'd shared with her sister earlier that night.

Within minutes of the 911 call, the Reine compound was swarming with police, state troopers from the crime-scene and ballistic units and homicide investigators from the Cape and Islands District Attorney's Office. As the phalanx of police vehicles set up outside, Domingues crumpled his small frame onto a curb. He shed no tears, but his fists were clenched tightly enough that his knuckles took on the pallor of the cranberries being harvested across the street. He pounded one of his fists into the concrete sidewalk over and over. Spectators to the chaos, mesmerized by the pandemonium of police lights and media trucks, gathered along the highway and stared at the small man on the curb whispering to himself, "Todd and Melvin did this. Todd and Melvin did this." He has since denied he said this, but spectators have confirmed the police version.

Domingues' rant would become a common refrain among the locals in Falmouth. "The boys," as Melvin Reine Sr.'s adult sons were referred to well after they'd both hit their late thirties and had children of their own, were quickly fingered as the likely culprits, the men with the motive and the means to do their stepmother harm. Melvin Jr. or "Melly" was 40, and known as the sweeter of the two. He had moved from the compound long before to raise his own family. Todd was 39 and had run up a rap sheet with the local police and earned a reputation for troublemaking.

The boys had been in a very public civil dispute with their stepmother for years, and there were allegations that they had tried to strong-arm her into signing over Five Star Enterprises to them. In fact, on the day of Shirley's murder, her attorney, William Enright, went as far as to publicly accuse the boys of setting up the hit. Enright noted that Shirley had been slated to face Melvin Jr. and Todd in ten days as the defendant in a lawsuit titled *Reine v. Reine* over control of the trash business and other family assets. The brothers claimed their stepmother had duped their father into putting his lucrative estate in her name while he suffered from dementia, and that she had stolen property that was rightfully theirs. Shirley Reine had countered that she'd run the company without her stepsons for years. Besides, she told the court in an affidavit, she was personally wounded by the idea that the suit had even been filed by the men she had watched over since they were children, saying, "I helped raise the plaintiffs and was their de facto mother since they were about the ages of five and six." It was an argument she would never get to make in court. However, Shirley Reine failed to indicate that she'd become the boys' "de facto mother" only after their own mother vanished in 1971 under suspicious circumstances. Investigators believe Melvin Reine Sr. made the boys' mother vanish and then took up with the 16-year-old babysitter—who happened to be Shirley Reine, who was Souza before she married Reine.

Wanda Reine's disappearance was considered by many people in Falmouth to be the first of several crimes— homicides, violent attacks and arson fires—that her husband Melvin Sr. would be eyed for. But because her body was never found, he was never charged. It was one of the many crimes that Melvin Reine would escape prosecution for during the decades that he had Falmouth under his firm control, Massachusetts police and district attorneys now believe.

Shirley's sister, Loretta Gilfoy, could not help thinking about Wanda every time she visited the Reine compound, which was rarely. Over the years, she had grown to like the elder Reine, and accepted the fact that her sister loved the old coot. But the picture of Wanda that police circulated as part of a missing persons report flashed in her mind as she pulled up to the crime scene where her sister had been shot dead. Sure, Loretta had heard the stories about Melvin Reine Sr.—"the Falmouth Fox" as he called himself, largely because he felt he consistently outfoxed local law enforcement and got away with an impressive swath of criminal activity. "I just never thought it would get this bad," she murmured to herself as she climbed out of the car, stunned and emotionless after getting a call from Michael Domingues.

She sat next to Domingues on the curb and wordlessly quieted him with a swift shake of her head when he began to talk about the Reine boys. It was something that they would discuss in a less public setting. "Someone was in there waiting for her. They followed her in, slipped underneath the door. She was shot getting out of her car, so somebody knew her exact schedule," Loretta mused.

Investigators doubted that Shirley Reine had gotten a good look at her killer. Within minutes of the police response, it became clear that the assassination of the attractive 51-year-old businesswoman had all the makings of a professional hit. The shots had been fired from close range by someone who may have had a gun equipped with a silencer. No ballistic evidence or fingerprints were found. No one in the extended Reine family had heard the shots. No one noticed if a strange vehicle had sped from the scene.

As the crime scene was processed, members of the Reine family stared out from windows of the other homes on the property. The garage windows became caked with white filmy fingerprint dust. Bags of evidence were carted away from inside the home. The garage door kicked from its hinges was tagged and bagged by crime-scene collectors wearing gloves on their hands and white booties over their own shoes to make sure no evidence was contaminated. Detectives fanned out into the crowd to interview potential witnesses. The house was ringed with yellow tape reading POLICE. DO NOT CROSS. There was a certain intentness to the cops' movements. They were being watched carefully by the neighbors, and every move would be broadcast on the local news.

Of course, any time a wealthy white woman is murdered in an upscale resort town like Falmouth—not only a summertime destination for scads of vacationers, but also the location of the ferry that shuttles the well-heeled and famous to Nantucket and Martha's Vineyard—the media descends. And the Cape and Islands had marked a strange spike in those kinds of killings in the years before Shirley Reine was slain. In the fall of 2004, Nantucket saw its first murder in twenty years: the stabbing of 44-year-old wealthy businesswoman Elizabeth Lochtefeld. An artist from a wealthy philanthropist family, Lochtefeld had fled an abusive boyfriend in New York City, only to have him follow her to a rented bungalow where he slaughtered her with a fishing knife. Massachusetts State Troopers who made the trip to Falmouth to work the Reine case had planned to spend the day tracking leads on the unsolved murder of pretty 23-year-old Kelly Ford, whose headless body was found buried on a Cape Cod beach in Sandwich in November 2001, two months after she'd vanished on her way to a job interview. And just about every investigator on the Cape had worked the murder of Christa Worthington, the former fashion writer who was stabbed to death in her family's Truro cottage in 2002, her toddler, Ava, desperately trying to nurse from her mother's bloodied, lifeless body.

Cape and Islands District Attorney Michael O'Keefe held a brief press conference about the murder of Shirley Reine at his office in Hyannis with Falmouth Police Chief David Cusolito at his side. O'Keefe did not take questions. "At approximately five thirty a.m., May 10, 2005, a family member called police and rescue units to respond to 657 East Falmouth Highway, Route 28, East Falmouth. Falmouth police and rescue units responded and found Shirley M. Reine, age fifty-one, deceased in her garage. Preliminary indications are that the cause of death is a gunshot wound to the head. The matter is being investigated as a criminal act perpetrated by another. The case is under investigation by the Falmouth police and the state police detective unit assigned to the district attorney's office. Also responding to the scene were crime-scene services and ballistics experts from the Massachusetts State Police." It was, however, what was not said at the press conference that was more telling. O'Keefe had a mess on his hands with this murder.

As investigators methodically processed the crime scene at Shirley Reine's house, they knew that their lives had just been disrupted by an around-the-clock case. Sleep would be scant, family lives nonexistent, kids' ball games missed as the officers grappled with a "media case," as high-profile murders are dubbed by police. Unrelenting media coverage inevitably led to public pressure from City Hall and police brass to make a quick arrest. Detectives were now not only tasked with solving the case, they also had to assuage the fears of Falmouth residents that Shirley Reine had been targeted at random by a homicidal lunatic, and had to send a strong message to the tourists who sustain the town's economy each summer that the situation was under control.

But Falmouth police knew that Shirley Reine had not been targeted by a crazy killer, and they knew tourists had nothing to worry about aside from the usual vacation nuisances like mosquitoes, high gas prices and parking tickets. It was not lost on some observers to the chaos that when they'd pulled up in front of the Reine compound, Falmouth cops had exchanged wry, worried looks. The old-timers on the force knew that Shirley Reine's murder was not a domestic violence case or a home invasion turned deadly. The concerned glances between gritty veterans had come with the knowledge that Shirley Reine's slaying could expose a long history of unsolved murders, police corruption and political pandering that could blow up the insular society that had long controlled Falmouth.

Just hours after Shirley Reine's murder, State Trooper Kris Bohnenberger had even written Todd Reine a traffic summons for driving to endanger. Todd Reine had nearly backed into the trooper at high speed—and when he saw that he'd almost hit a cop, Reine flipped Bohnenberger the finger. Somehow, though, the ticket was quashed before it ever made it to court, a move indicative of the hold the Reine family still had over the town of Falmouth years after the patriarch had been institutionalized.

The Falmouth cops also knew that blaming the Reine boys was almost too easy in a case with a legion of people with possible motives.

Just a few years earlier, those very cops had executed a raid on Shirley Reine's home that turned up not only an illegal .357 Magnum listed on the search warrant, but a box of sex tapes featuring Shirley pleasuring prominent Cape Cod men, men who may have received blackmail threats from the raven-haired beauty. By then, Shirley had also been fingered as an accomplice in the attempted murder of a Falmouth cop who'd suffered three blasts to the face, fired by Melvin's shotgun.

That case had remained a complete mystery on the Cape for decades. The maimed cop, John Busby, and his family were relocated to a small town in the South because he did not trust his comrades in the Falmouth Police Department. In fact, Busby had whispered Melvin Reine's name as his shooter through his mangled mouth in the emergency room the night of the attack, but the investigation had gone nowhere until Reine's brother came forward and confessed to being the getaway driver for the Falmouth Fox. By then, the statute of limitations had expired, and Melvin Reine would escape criminal charges once again. The disfigured cop had at one point vowed revenge, but has since taken up his cause to extend the statute of limitations for crimes against police officers.

Untold numbers of Falmouth residents were still infuriated about the land Reine and her husband used as a dump, leading to accusations that dirty deals had been made at the highest level of town government. Then there was the mysterious unsolved murder of a 16-year-old Falmouth boy who had developed a crush on Shirley Reine. Her husband was the last person to have seen him alive before his bullet-riddled body was pulled from the marsh behind the Reine compound. There was also the unexplained disappearance of a 17-year-old Five Star Enterprises employee who'd vanished days before he was scheduled to testify against Melvin Reine Sr. in an arson case. A Falmouth cop had escorted him to a ferryboat bound for Martha's Vineyard, but the teen never arrived on the island and his body has never been found. Even Domingues' wife was on the list of potential suspects, and police questioned her about where she was the night Shirley was killed. She had engaged in a public squabble with Shirley Reine in the weeks before the murder, during which threats were issued.

Those in the small town also tittered about the substantial loan Shirley Reine and her husband had made to a Cape Cod restaurateur who enjoyed boasting of his mob connections, money that the dead woman had demanded back in the months before she was killed. Even the Falmouth police force could not be entirely ruled out. Falmouth Police Captain Roman "Skip" Medeiros was one of the first officers at the murder scene that morning, but he was forced to remove himself from the case after he was questioned and his connection to the deceased was exposed. After all, his little sister Wanda had been Melvin Reine Sr.'s first wife, who'd disappeared in 1971, abandoning her children, an act that her family knew was unfathomable for the devoted mother. Melvin, Medeiros knew, had waited five days to report Wanda missing, and told police a rambling story about how he had dropped her off at a bus depot and never heard from her again. Even more than thirty years after the disappearance, there was still bad blood between Medeiros and the Reine clan. From the start, Wanda's family had suspected foul play. Shirley Reine had moved into Melvin's home to take care of the kids after Wanda went missing. It didn't take long for her to move into Melvin's bed.

After most murders, homicide investigators focus on who would have a reason to kill the victim. But with the Shirley Reine case, they would have to figure out who didn't.

Sure, there was a long list of suspects in Shirley Reine's murder. But the blasts that opened up her chest and created a bloodbath in her garage had further-reaching implications. Her killing sparked new questions about the crimes her husband had long been suspected of. More important for Falmouth police officers both active and retired, there would be a new look at how one man was able to corrupt so many law enforcement officials to help him maintain a firm grasp of violence in a seemingly peaceful New England town.

TWO

Wanda "Tudy" Medeiros was just a teenager when she became enamored with Melvin Reine. A shy, bespectacled girl, she was intrigued by the older bad boy, the man who had a reputation around town that he should not be messed with.

Reine was not particularly good-looking. He had skin already leathery from the sun, even though he was in his early twenties. He had a strong, stocky build, but barely stood five-foot-eight-inches tall and only weighed 160 pounds at his heaviest. He was given to strange, inappropriate grinning that made some people wonder if he was simple-minded. His dark hair was usually shellacked back on his head with gel, or tousled as if he hadn't showered in days. It was his eyes that really unsettled people, however. He would usually do one of two things: stare intently or completely avert any eye contact at all. Either was odd.

Wanda, on the other hand, was prim and distinguished in comparison. Smart and well-read, Wanda was raised as one of eight children in a tight-knit Portuguese family that put a lot of emphasis on outward appearance and believed that young ladies should conduct themselves with poise. Even if she'd wanted to behave like the fast girls in Falmouth, Wanda had overprotective older brothers who not only made sure the hems of her skirts fell below her knees and that her sweaters were loosely fitting, but intimidated any local boy who wanted to ask their slight little sister out on a date.

Melvin Reine was not intimidated by anyone. He would not be deterred from pursuing Wanda, the town "good girl," even if the Medeiros brothers were robustly built and quick with their hands. He wasn't bothered that they came from the bloodline of a law-enforcement family and he was a well-known town thug.

Wanda's brother Roman had known since he was a child that his calling was police work, and it was only a matter of time before he was sworn onto the Falmouth force, a fact that stymied most of the tough guys in town from trying to provoke him—everyone, that is, but Melvin Reine. It also meant that Roman was privy to persistent rumors about Reine's hot temper and knew that it could flare up without warning. He also knew that Reine was considered a crime lord of sorts by investigators and that he had insinuated ties to organized crime syndicates. The truth was that Reine had ruled over a group of dysfunctional, miscreant teenagers who were years younger than he was. The Medeiroses knew way too much about the "Falmouth Fox," and would impress the fact that he was "no good" onto their daughter over and over again. The admonitions from her overprotective family undoubtedly fueled Wanda's infatuation with Melvin.

Initially, their love affair was a clandestine one, stealing kisses on the rickety docks behind Melvin's family compound, or walking around Bourne's Pond, which was right before the bend in Route 28 that had become known as Reine's Corner. Reine's parents, Manuel and Adeline, were also strict, and, having grown up laboring as cranberry pickers, had raised their five children to know the value of hard work. But it was not difficult for Melvin and Wanda to sneak around. The Medeiros house was not far from the Reine compound, a short walk up a steep hill, on the thoroughfare across from an old firehouse.

Wanda's mother Mary and her father Manuel were beside themselves about the affair. There were sometimes tensions between Cape Verdean clans like Reine's and those of Portuguese backgrounds like the Medeiroses. The friction between the two groups did not make much sense, given that both cultures were so similar, cherishing family and fishing above all else. In fact, extended members of Reine's Cape

Verdean family would sit alongside some of the Medeiros clan on Sundays at St. Anthony's Church—the one place in town where Cape Verdeans and Portuguese families commingled without incident.

But it was not Reine's culture that had the Medeiros family up in arms. Their biggest concern was that Melvin Reine would not be much of a provider for a young woman. After all, at 25 he was barely literate, with a seventh-grade education and an IQ that tested at 50, who drove a trash truck for a living. A man who could not look anyone in the eye, and when he did, most wished he wouldn't. Certainly no one ever predicted that Melvin Reine would one day own one of the biggest trash-hauling companies on Cape Cod.

The minute Wanda turned 18, her parents no longer had a hold over her, and she accepted Melvin Reine's marriage proposal. There was no diamond engagement ring. No wedding fanfare. Her family was so angry that they refused to plan an elaborate reception or even attend a church service. Melvin Reine wasn't bothered when he was shunned. He loaded Wanda into a borrowed trash truck and the two drove to City Hall in the college town of Dartmouth, Massachusetts, where they were married by a justice of the peace on October 26, 1964.

Seven years later, Melvin would take Wanda on another ride—only this time she would never be seen again.

THREE

Wanda's strained relationship with her mother Mary began to repair itself naturally with the birth of the Reines' first son, Melvin "Melly" Reine Jr., which came two years after the couple had exchanged vows. The birth of that baby helped Mary resolve her resentment and release the sense of impending doom that nagged at her every time she thought of her daughter's marriage. Instead, Mary Medeiros focused on her duties as a grandmother, helping Wanda during the early months of motherhood.

When Todd was born a year after Melly, Wanda not only relied on her mother for help with her two babies, she needed her for simple companionship. By then, her husband was anywhere but home. He was working around the clock, or hanging out with young teenagers in shopping center parking lots. But this was okay with Wanda, because she was anxiety-ridden when her husband was around. He was so volatile, so prone to angry outbursts that she was relieved when he stayed out. She focused on raising their little boys and wanted to make sure that they did not follow in their father's footsteps. Sure, Melvin Reine was a provider, a worker. But there was also a palpable simmering rage in him, a character flaw that Wanda prayed nightly her boys would not inherit.

Finally, he would be out of the home for more than a year and a half—a period that Wanda would come to regard as the most peaceful time of her life. The absence was not planned, but instead would come with Melvin Reine's first—and last—criminal conviction, which would send him to Walpole, the most volatile prison in the Massachusetts Department of Correction.

The winter of 1968 was a time of total chaos in Falmouth. In the late 1960s, the town was centered on its villages: East Falmouth, Teaticket, Woods Hole, the Center, West Falmouth and North Falmouth. Located on the southwestern tip of Cape Cod, Falmouth is just three miles from the island of Martha's Vineyard and noted by sea captains from all over the world for its brilliant lighthouse, Nobska Light. In the 1970s, Falmouth would see a housing boom spawned by the construction of the military base Camp Edwards. But until then, Falmouth was home to summer people from Memorial Day to Labor Day, who left when the chill began to set in, with brisk winds off the shores and a type of bracing cold tolerated only by the heartiest of New Englanders. Laborers who settled there after spending a grueling season harvesting cranberries or picking strawberries for the Boston market were the only year-round residents. A strong sense of community and family helped Falmouth eventually burgeon into the bustling resort town it is today.

Falmouth would eventually become famous after the discovery of the sunken hull of the doomed *Titanic*, as the treasure hunt that followed was centralized in Falmouth. Ball players from the famed Cape Cod Baseball League—considered by many sports aficionados as a farm team for the majors—have played in Falmouth parks since 1885 and often live with families there. Historians point out that Falmouth was settled by Quakers in 1660 and incorporated by a whaling and sheep-herding town eight years later. Today its Village Green is still a quaint grassy patch with a backdrop of historic homes and a whitewashed church. It is "the essence of a New England town," the Falmouth Chamber of Commerce boasts.

But in 1968, Falmouth still maintained its small-town American feel, where neighbors watched other neighbors' children and police officers knew everyone in the community. Falmouth was always a wonderful place to raise a family, which is why so many people come with a plan to visit for a short summer break and then decide to stay for good.

The reason Falmouth became so popular went beyond its sense of community. It is also staggeringly beautiful, with miles of cranberry bogs, and white-capped waves crashing on champagne-colored sandy beaches. It was never hard to imagine why the town's most famous native, the legendary poet Katharine Lee Bates, who was born in Falmouth in 1859, called on her childhood on the Cape when she penned the hymn "America the Beautiful." She had scribbled the lyrics down in a notebook when she was 34 years old and far from Cape Cod, but there is no doubt that her memories of Falmouth inspired the hymn.

So when flames began to light up the pitch-dark winter skies on the morning side of midnight that February of 1968, the residents of Falmouth were terrified. The fires were intentionally set. And the arsonist had to be a local.

The summer residents had boarded up waterfront cottages months before, and rarely did day-trippers trek to the bracingly cold shorelines of Cape Cod in the dead of winter. Firefighters, many of them volunteers or "vollies" with full-time day jobs, battled a dozen blazes over a three-week period. Fighting fires in the cold is particularly dangerous: hoses freeze; the icy ground is perilous. Valiant searches for victims were required to be conducted even in mansions and businesses considered closed for the winter, as there was no way to be sure that someone had not holed up in a boarded building to escape the cold. Each time the fire bell rang, wives sucked in a nervous breath as their husbands pulled on their protective bunker gear. Firefighters said a silent prayer to the God of their understanding. It was clear that accelerants had been used to set each of the blazes. The smell of kerosene or gasoline is impossible to mask, and when that odor smacked their nostrils, worried firefighters became even sharper at the scenes. Arson fires fueled by accelerants could easily culminate with a dangerous flashover—or backdraft—explosion, a condition that could come without warning. The potential for any one of the firebug's crimes to become deadly was there every time flames erupted.

Firefighters who had to break icicles off their helmets and pull their gloves off frozen hoses to avoid frostbite did not have time to pay attention to the spectators who crowded behind the police tape stretched around the scene. If they had, they might have noticed a man with an unsettling smirk curled on his lips, his dead, dark eyes darting over the chaos with a strange sense of glee. That man went unnoticed—at first. But at the third or fourth fire scene, cops and firefighters exchanged looks with one another and nodded their heads when one of them mouthed, *Is that Melvin Reine?* It was.

Reine did not care that people noticed him. He could feel their rage, their fear, their hatred. He enjoyed taunting everyone in the town. It seared his reputation as the Falmouth Fox into the minds of anyone who dared antagonize or challenge him. And that included the town's police force. He even had the gall to remark to a cop, "You have to catch this guy. He's crazy."

It was no secret that Reine had long used fire as an intimidation tool. If he had a beef with someone, he would strike a match and fling it on the ground at the feet of whoever he was feuding with. Or else he would simply mutter under his breath, "I smell smoke." Sometimes he grinned like a lunatic and yelped, "It's getting hot around here." It was not long after any of those threats were delivered that the smell of charred wood would waft through Falmouth as flames ripped through a mansion, a business, a motel or a summer cottage in one of Falmouth's villages.

No one was too powerful to escape Reine's wrath. A legendary Mashpee cop named Fred Bohnenberger, who'd pulled him over for a traffic violation—in defiance of the tacit amnesty granted by many of the cops, who had become terrified of the Falmouth Fox—was the recipient of one of Reine's arson threats. Reine took the ticket, stared intently into the cop's eyes and snarled, "It's going to get hot at your house, Fred." Bohnenberger, who was incorruptible, told Reine that threats would do nothing to deter him from carrying out his duty. Melvin Reine never attacked Bohnenberger's house, but he did undermine the cop's ability to do his job. Bohnenberger's boss would consistently quash tickets that were written to Melvin Reine. And, in what would become a pattern for the local police departments, rank-and-file officers who did not feel supported by their superiors would become just as apathetic as the bosses.

In order to send a message to police forces that the Fox was a force to be reckoned with, Reine set fire to then–Falmouth Police Chief John Ferreira's personal car, and laughed as it burned in his driveway. Cops would later say that Ferreira came outside and saw Reine parked across the street, enjoying the fright he had invoked on the face of the highest-ranking law enforcement official in the town.

The fires—especially Ferreira's torched car—thrilled Melvin Reine well beyond the sense of power that comes to most arsonists when mayhem is created. It was not the shrill screech of fire engines or the frantic efforts of emergency responders that gave him the biggest high. Reine knew that his arrogant crime spree had managed to make most of the young police officers on the Falmouth force afraid of him; it cemented his reputation for outfoxing the law. Reine had always been a thug and a troublemaker in town. But this was different. It was clear he had no boundaries, and did not fear the law. There were fewer than a dozen full-time Falmouth police officers—the force was bolstered by specially hired cops in the summer—and now all of them knew that Reine was capable of anything. Certainly not many of the underpaid officers were willing to take a bullet or a chance that their families could burn to death just so they could bust Reine's chops with a traffic citation or criminal investigation. Others were simply dirty and had developed friendships or business deals with Melvin Reine. One cop had even been spotted acting as Reine's chauffeur—in a marked Falmouth police cruiser.

The state trooper assigned to handle the arson investigation was an outsider named Robert Enos. Enos had heard of the Falmouth Fox from other state police who worked Cape Cod barracks, but he was no townie and he was certainly not going to allow a small-time hood to intimidate him. He quietly began to gather intelligence, careful not to share too much information with the Falmouth cops. He began to interview people close to Melvin Reine, including a misfit teen who had moved into the Reine compound weeks earlier after a fight with his own family. That would provide the break police needed in the case.

That teen would later describe for a jury exactly what happened the night he and Reine set the first fire at a palatial waterfront estate, a summer home used by wealthy Bostonians nestled among the sand not far from Nobska Light. In all, seven seasonal homes would be destroyed during the three-week spree.

The *Cape Cod Times* described that first mansion fire this way:

> On a winter night in 1968, Melvin Reine and a teenage friend cruised across town toward Nobska Light. Reine, then 27, got out of the car as the teen looked on. He poured kerosene on the breezeway walls of the empty Fay Road mansion. He struck a match and lit the gas. Flames crawled up the shingled summer home as Reine jumped into his car and the pair drove away. He warned the teen to keep his mouth shut because he was just as guilty for being there. Sirens and fire whistles blared as regular and call firefighters rushed to the scene. And as firefighters scrambled to extinguish the blaze, a crowd gathered to watch. Among them was Reine.

He was even audacious enough to spew braggadocio about the fires police were now sure he had been setting. "I'll talk to the bug and I'll let you know when the next fire is going to be," Reine remarked to various townsfolk. He also continued to taunt police with questions like "Why can't you find the bug?" In the meantime, a beachfront hotel closed for the winter, Shorehaven Motor Lodge, burned to the ground. A vacant building owned by a Falmouth police officer was torched. A lumber yard owned by a Reine rival was taken out.

Enos had conducted enough counter-surveillance working with the state police investigators assigned to the Cape and Islands District Attorney's Office that he already noted that Melvin Reine had admired every pre-dawn fire. He hadn't missed a single one. Reine was so brazen that investigators would spot him in the crowd and needle him for information.

"What do you think started this one, Melvin?" Falmouth firefighter and arson investigator Frederick "Chip" Crocker would ask.

Reine would have an answer without even a slight hesitation. His ego would not allow him to stay silent, even if it meant he was giving Crocker information easily confirmed by State Police Crime Lab experts, information that would help implicate him in the crimes.

"I think it was kerosene and cardboard," Reine answered. "Yeah. I think the bug used kerosene and cardboard this time."

Crocker did not let Reine's arrogance deter him. It was only a matter of time before he and Bobby Enos would nail Reine. In fact, the teenager who'd helped Reine at a number of fire scenes had already started to break. The next time Reine mocked any of the investigators by asking, "How come you can't catch the bug?" Enos just smiled.

Don't worry, Melvin, Enos thought, *we will.*

It was Reine's bravado that would ultimately doom him. Melvin Reine was a grown man, a 27-year-old married man with two kids, in fact, yet he still spent his nights drinking beer in local parking lots with teenagers. Like most criminals, Reine was maniacally narcissistic. There was no way he could pull off something as blatant as the systematic burning of a dozen properties if no one appreciated his criminal prowess. He needed a witness, a cohort. Someone he could brag about the fires with. He tapped the troubled 17-year-old who had left a dysfunctional family and moved in with the Reines. That teen would come to be the only witness who ever cooperated with police against Reine to live to tell the tale. Years later, he would recall his own fear to the *Cape Cod Times*, with the caveat that the reporter would vow to protect his anonymity.

"I knew Melvin was going to throw me under the bus, and I wanted to go into the Army, go into the Guard and get out of Falmouth," the teen told the reporter. He then went on to describe how Reine would pour kerosene or gasoline on piles of newspapers and strike a match. When the flames grew, Reine would smirk and find "a place to watch them, or went right back to the scene to watch them."

Enos arrested Reine on the night of February 28, 1968, with the assistance of a Falmouth police officer named Daniel Cunha, who had grown up just a few houses away from the Reine compound. It was one of those New England nights when a late winter storm had coated the roadways with a wet, messy slush. Reine had landed a lucrative contract from the town of Falmouth to plow city streets, a job that raised the ire of honest, hardworking people who had never had a chance to even bid on the job. Falmouth selectmen would never explain how Reine had received that contract—or the one to haul trash—despite a criminal history. Cunha tracked down Melvin Reine and yanked him from the driver's seat of his snow plow.

It felt good to slap the cuffs on Reine's slight wrists. Cunha registered the stunned look on the Falmouth Fox's face, and for a second he smiled before reading Reine his rights. Reine could set the chief's car on fire. He could torch another cop's business without repercussion. But no one was going to get away with laughing in Cunha's face the way Reine had done so many nights during the three-week arson spree.

Who's laughing now, Melvin? Cunha remembered thinking.

Cunha was young and single. He was not going to let a guy like Melvin Reine prevent him from being a cop, or more important, a man.

Reine was arraigned at Barnstable District Court on March 1, 1968, and charged with seven counts of arson. There had been a total of twelve fires, but the chief inexplicably did not want to press charges. The other five blazes had left too much damage and not enough evidence. Cunha explained the charges against Reine this way: "He was charged with what we could prove."

It was clear that investigators were convinced that Reine had set all twelve fires during the arson spree, but they were grateful to have gotten an arrest warrant for the seven. As predicted, he tried to blame the teenager for all the fires. Reine even stood up in court and declared that he was an innocent man. He was not the firebug—he was just another citizen victimized by the psycho setting the fires.

"There was a fire back of our house, about a quarter mile. The trucks were on their way to fight the fire. I got so mad about it, I went to help find the firebug," Reine said during his court proceeding.

The court didn't buy Reine's story. He was convicted on seven counts of arson and sentenced to 5 to 8 years in a state prison on April 25, 1968.

Astonishingly enough, Melvin Reine had logged another arrest while he was awaiting trial. He was accused by police of having an illicit affair with a teenager who would become pregnant. The teen's parents called police. Melvin Reine was arrested again and charged with two counts of statutory rape and two counts of lewd and lascivious behavior. The bail he posted in connection with the arson cases was revoked. But Reine got lucky in that one. A grand jury heard the case against him and decided there was no probable cause to proceed.

Melvin Reine was apparently a very lucky man. In fact, during the years before he had been convicted of the arson, he had built up an impressive rap sheet that stretched back more than a decade. His first arrest had come on larceny charges in 1956, for which he received a suspended sentence. A year later he was busted for driving with a suspended license and paid a $50 fine. In 1966, he was arrested for not paying child support for one of his many illegitimate children. (Falmouth's community newspaper, *The Enterprise*, reported in 2005 that Melvin Reine had fathered a total of thirty-eight children on Cape Cod. Investigators I spoke to say Reine has "dozens" of illegitimate children.) He was found not guilty and it was unclear if he was even forced to pay up what he owed to the single mom. He was arrested again in January of 1968 for larceny, another case that for some bizarre reason was not prosecuted. Court records cited that the case was dismissed because there was no probable cause, a pattern that would continue throughout Melvin Reine's long life of tangling with the law. Investigators poring over Melvin Reine's criminal history in the days after his second wife Shirley was killed would be puzzled by the form known in Massachusetts as the CORI (Criminal Offender Registry Information) because of what appeared to be intervention from some level of law enforcement to get Reine off the hook for a plethora of serious crimes, including rape. In the decades after his arson conviction, Reine would be arrested nearly a dozen times on charges that included the attempted murder of a police officer, but every time, his cases were dismissed by the court—sometimes without even a notification to the arresting officer, which is standard practice in criminal proceedings.

Reine's luck would continue. The arson conviction would be Melvin Reine's first—and last—experience in the Massachusetts penal system. Sure, Reine was stunned when the jury came back with a guilty verdict. He was shocked when the judge actually handed him the harsh sentence of 5 to 8 years. He knew no crooked cop, no amount of political pull or underworld juice could get him out of a conviction to state prison.

But Massachusetts has a national reputation as a state that coddles convicts. Somehow Reine's stiff sentence was shaved down to a year and a half, a shock to the police and prosecutors who'd worked hard to put him away. The first 90 days of that sentence was spent at Bridgewater, a prison for the mentally ill. He was given a psychiatric evaluation there, and a psychologist determined that for Reine, setting fires not only provided a sense of power, but also gave him "extreme sexual arousal." His Department of Correction file made note of the compulsion to light fires and the turn-on it provided before Reine was shipped off to Walpole, the most notoriously violent prison in Massachusetts.

The teenaged accomplice whose testimony had nailed Reine served 6 months in a county jail. Two years after his release, his new Pontiac convertible went up in flames in the driveway of his Cape Cod home. Melvin Reine had only been out of prison for days when the car was burned.

"Melvin used to go by and wave, and that was a wave of, like, is he going to shoot me the next time he sees me? I was afraid of what could happen," the teen said.

He had reason to be afraid. Melvin Reine just honed his dark side while serving time among rapists, pedophiles, killers and urban gang members at Walpole. It was a place where men were broken by ceaseless bloodletting and brutal sexual assaults. It was not a pleasant place even for the most hardscrabble con. While Melvin Reine was a tough guy in Falmouth, the Cape Cod villages were not exactly as rough-and-tumble as the city of Boston's grittiest neighborhoods. He was no match for hardcore gangbangers and remorseless men who had slaughtered their own wives and children. Those men had no souls and did not care about consequences behind bars for attacking a newbie to the system. The system did not rehabilitate Melvin Reine. It just hardened him.

Reine spent the last ninety days of his sentence doing hard labor on a farm at the Plymouth County Correctional Facility. He preferred scooping cow dung to avoiding attack, and was grateful that he was moving around. The prison officials sent Reine to the minimum security farm detail as a test. If he behaved, they could push him out of the overcrowded prison system and put him under parole supervision back on the streets of Falmouth. He passed the test and would be going home a lot earlier than anyone thought.

But by then, the time he'd spent in Walpole had already done its damage.

Melvin Reine had been a disturbed man long before he saw the inside of a cell at Walpole State Prison. But after he'd served hard time alongside the most vile and violent inmates in the state, Melvin Reine came home downright deranged.

FOUR

Wanda Medeiros and her family were hoping that her husband would never get out of jail, or better yet, he might fall victim to a terrible accident delivered by an inmate wielding the wrong end of a sharpened toothbrush. It had become peaceful in the Reine compound without Melvin. People in the supermarket had stopped avoiding Wanda in the aisle. Policemen who once passed by without acknowledgment now gave her a friendly wave. Other children invited Melly and Todd to birthday parties. Mothers began to chat with her outside the school. Without Melvin, she was just another neighbor in a town that was known as a great place to live, work and raise a family. She was not just the wife of the Falmouth Fox; Wanda had matured into her own woman. She was a mother and a community member without Melvin Reine's baggage.

With Melvin incarcerated, Wanda and her mother had become best friends. All that awkwardness that was created between Wanda and her brothers when she'd married Melvin had dissipated. Best of all, at least to Wanda, that panic that accompanied Melvin's daily mid-morning return to the house was gone. She had stopped holding her breath every time she heard a truck's tires crush against the smashed clamshells in the driveway leading to the business behind her house. The tension lines between her brows relaxed.

But liberal Massachusetts is notorious for lenient sentences, and there was a time that no one in the state served a sentence to its full term. The 5- to 8-year reprieve Wanda thought she had received when her husband was convicted was a farce. She did not even receive an alert from her husband or the Department of Correction when they first allowed Melvin into a work camp on Cape Cod. Then one winter day in 1970, Melvin Reine came home. He had called his brother John for a ride. One bitterly cold afternoon, Wanda Reine heard the crunch of seashells in her driveway. She pulled back the lace curtain and gasped when she saw Melvin in the car with her brother-in-law. He had not even been gone for two years. Wanda watched all of her problems climb out with Melvin as he pulled his small frame out of the car. He smiled as he walked in the door.

And when the door shut behind him, it would only take minutes for Wanda to realize that Melvin Reine had brought a whole new kind of chaos with him.

He had decided that Wanda should have some household help, a nanny for the boys. That babysitter happened to be their leggy 16-year-old neighbor. Shirley Souza had grown up across the street from the Reine compound. As a girl, she was chubby and clumsy, and her teeth jutted out of her mouth in an overbite. Her skin was marred with acne and she was terribly shy. She went largely unnoticed by Melvin Reine until he returned from Walpole. During the eighteen months he'd been away, Shirley Souza had grown into a buxom teenager. She had slimmed out in the hips and belly, with her extra weight transferred to her breasts and behind. Shirley had the same black hair and wide smile as his wife, but preferred inappropriately short miniskirts and tight tank tops. She was known around town as a spitfire who would toss around her long, curly black hair seductively. She had none of the hang-ups that Wanda had been raised with about inappropriate dress or lewd behavior. Shirley Souza knew what her assets were and flaunted them accordingly with her wardrobe.

Wanda was no dummy, and she noticed each time her husband's glance lingered on the younger girl's figure. Calling Shirley a family babysitter was a misnomer, as her services were almost never required. Wanda had never left her sons alone in the years since they had been born. Besides, Shirley Souza would be the last person Wanda would entrust with her children's well-being. But each time she protested about Shirley spending more and more time at the house, Melvin responded wordlessly with the scowl that gave Wanda an anxiety attack. Back was her shortness of breath. Wanda's own skin took on the yellowing pallor of old newspaper. It did not take long for Melvin to settle into his old pattern of womanizing and working. Even if Wanda did not see much of him, when she did see him, he managed to bring back that all-too-familiar feeling of incessant panic. She sought solace in her mother's company—and in spending time with her boys.

On the morning of March 12, 1971, Wanda took her sons shopping with their grandmother. Mary Medeiros would later remember how she'd stolen a long look at her daughter in the sun and wondered how Wanda had come to look so old.

Wanda was only 25, but she had taken on the look of an elderly widow. On that March day she wore her horn-rimmed glasses and a simple string of pearls, with her hair cropped tight around her head in a matronly helmet. She had on a salmon-colored skirt that fell to her knees, a three-quarter-length navy blue raincoat, and her flat buckled shoes—an ensemble that did nothing to accentuate her five-foot-six, 125-pound figure. Wanda was not bothered. It had been a long time since she and Melvin had exchanged any secret kisses like the ones of her youth. She had lost any zeal to be attractive. Besides, rumors were circulating that Melvin had already impregnated at least one woman in Falmouth, and may have even had a bevy of other love children being raised in another Cape Cod town. All of it left Wanda dog-tired. She could not even be bothered to care about her husband's philandering. She certainly could not bring herself to care about her sex appeal. Instead, she focused on raising her two sons to be studious and respectful. She refused to allow them to be written off by the town of Falmouth as no-good Reine boys like so many in the clan already had been. In keeping with her devotion to Todd and Melly, the only jewelry Wanda wore that day was her simple gold wedding band, a ring dotted with two rubies that had been her own grandmother's, and a mother's ring with two simple stones representing the births of her boys.

Mary Medeiros did not comment on her daughter's appearance on that March day, but it would nag at her, even years later. She hated the fact that Wanda was so unhappy and resisted the urge to lecture her. When Mary watched Wanda walk into the Reine compound with her grandsons as the sun set over the cranberry bogs, she had no way of knowing that it would be the last time she would ever see her daughter.

The women had fallen into a routine where Mary would wake up and call Wanda to chitchat about the day ahead. They never had much to talk about really, but Mary knew that her daughter did not have any friends, and that their morning phone calls kept Wanda connected to adults. On March 13, 1971, her grandson Melvin Jr. answered the phone.

"Hello, Melly," Mary murmured. "Where's your mother?"

"Isn't Mother with you?" the little boy said. "She went to see you last night. She got into father's blue truck and they went to see you. That's what Shirley said."

Mary was immediately alarmed. Her daughter had not spent a single moment away from their sons since they were born. Melvin was not capable of taking care of children. He was too busy working or networking with the friends he'd met at Walpole. Jail had hardened him—and not just with the prison muscles he'd developed that gave his body the shape of a compact bullet. Those eyes that had for years instilled fear in people were now dead—soulless. He looked at his sons as if he did not even see them. Certainly, Mary had not grown any fonder of her son-in-law. In her eyes he was still a shiftless punk with no future, who'd failed to fulfill his primary duty as a father to her grandsons. She did not care that Melvin Reine was on the verge of opening his own trash-hauling company, called Five Star Enterprises. Her daughter would become well-off financially, but emotionally Wanda was not well. Mary Medeiros never confronted Melvin Reine—since he'd returned from prison, she had grown afraid of him.

So when Wanda did not pick up the phone that morning, Mary's stomach fluttered with thoughts of what her daughter's husband was capable of. After sucking in a deep breath, she told her grandson to put his father on the phone.

"Melvin, where is my daughter?" Mary barked. "Melly said she came to see me, and she certainly did not. The last time I saw her was when we went shopping. You and I both know she would never come here without the boys."

"Mary, calm down. She went to go visit her cousin in Wareham," Melvin Reine said, referring to a town roughly twenty minutes away from their Falmouth home. "I dropped her off at the bus last night."

Mary wasn't buying that story. Nor did she buy the other explanation Melvin offered up. He claimed that he'd had a fight with her daughter, thrown $300 at her and told her to get out. That was utter nonsense, and Mary Medeiros told Melvin as much. That was when he changed his tune and came up with the bus ride to Wareham. That tale was just as bogus. The Medeiroses did not have any relatives in Wareham who Wanda would up and visit without warning, especially at night without the boys. In fact, the only family member who had ever lived in Wareham had moved six months earlier, a fact that had already come up at a family gathering. If Melvin Reine had shown up at any of the family gatherings at the Medeiros home, he would have known that already.

"Melvin, I know Tudy does not go anywhere without her children. Where is she?" Mary asked urgently. "We don't have cousins in Wareham. I am not going to let this go, Melvin Reine. I am calling the police."

Without saying a word, Melvin replaced the phone in its receiver and told his sons and the babysitter not to answer it again. Four days after Wanda vanished, Shirley Souza moved into the Reine compound. Melvin explained the odd living situation by saying that someone had to watch out for the children now that his wife had abandoned him. He mused aloud that Wanda had probably run off with another man. For her part, Shirley Souza told the boys in her care that their mother had gone to live with their grandmother, but could not explain why she had not called, why they could not go see her. That was a story she would repeat to the police, who showed up at the house on March 17, 1971—five days after Wanda had vanished. It would take Melvin Reine that long to file a missing persons report like the one that his mother-in-law had filed on March 13.

"She told me she was going to visit her mother," Shirley said under questioning from a Falmouth police detective before Melvin came into the house from an office located above the garage. Melvin could not explain why he had waited five days before calling the police to report his wife missing.

"Hey, she ran off or something. I don't need the whole town knowing my business," Melvin snarled to Falmouth Police Captain Leonard Martin. "I dropped her off to go on a vacation with her cousin. That's all I know. What? Why would I assume anything else was going on?

"I brought her to the bus station. She wanted to see her cousin. She was going to Wareham," Melvin Reine said.

Shirley Souza did not say a word. The story she'd told the detective about the visit to her mother's house conflicted with Melvin's. She knew she had flubbed up, and that Melvin was going to be angry, but it was too late to rectify the situation.

The story sounded flimsy to Captain Martin, and it was. Mary Medeiros had already alerted the Falmouth police to the cousin's move. And a simple check of the bus schedule at Falmouth's Woods Hole station would prove there had been no buses to Wareham on the afternoon in question. Police officers went as far as to show Wanda Reine's picture to bus station employees to see if anyone remembered seeing her. No one did. Mary Medeiros was not the only one convinced that her daughter had met with some kind of foul play at the hands of the "Falmouth Fox." Martin called Barnstable County

District Attorney Philip Rollins and the prosecutor called in the state police to handle the investigation. It was clear to the men that Wanda Reine had not strayed off.

None of them could help but notice there was a fresh concrete pour on Melvin's property.

"You're not going to let him outfox you again, are you?" Mary asked detectives through angry tears. She and her family had organized their own search parties to trudge through the marshy areas behind Melvin Reine's family compound and comb through the tall scraggly grass surrounding the nearby cranberry bogs. "I have thought this from the first day, and I hope to God it's not true, but Wanda is dead. Melvin did this. You can't let him get away with this."

Martin was one of the good guys in the Falmouth Police Department, with no ties to Reine or his relatives. That was not typically the case, as Reine had somehow managed to corrupt a surprising number of the police officers on the force. He did not pay parking tickets. No one in his bloodline ever faced arrest, even if they acted in a criminal manner. Martin had seen it happen himself where Reine strode into the Falmouth police headquarters, chatted with a cop and emerged with that eerie grin of his. That always meant a traffic violation had been quashed or a relative had been pulled out of a jam. Of course, all of this was after Reine had set the chief's car on fire, so the exchange was unsettling at best.

Martin did not respond to Mary Medeiros out loud, but instead told himself, *Enough is enough. This is a young woman with two little boys.* Martin's frustration with his fellow officers reached a crescendo when reports began to pile up on his desk that suggested Wanda had in fact abandoned her family for another man. One report detailed a phone call purportedly placed to the Falmouth police station on March 21. The caller stated that she was Wanda Reine and that she wanted to assuage any panic in the town. "She said she was all right and wanted to know what all the fuss was about," according to the report.

"There is no reason to be worried," the woman who

claimed to be Wanda Reine told the Falmouth officer who answered her call. "I'm fine." Or at least that is what the Falmouth officer claimed on the report.

On that same day, Melvin Reine called Martin and reported getting an identical call from Wanda.

"She wanted to know what all the commotion was about," Reine told the detective.

Then there was a third call placed to a friend of Wanda's. That caller told the friend's employee, "There is nothing to worry about."

But Martin wasn't buying any of it. In fact, he was convinced that the teenaged babysitter, Shirley, may have been the one making the phone calls. After all, Wanda Reine did not call her son Melly on his birthday, or her own mother on Mother's Day. That cast doubts on any idea that she'd placed calls to a husband she hated, an acquaintance and the Falmouth police. Not likely. When Martin told Melvin Reine that the phone calls were malarkey, the Falmouth Fox just grinned.

"The cops drive by Wanda every day," he said. "You just don't see her."

That taunt set in motion a series of searches. Martin did not think the freshly poured concrete in Melvin Reine's garage was a coincidence. Backhoes had also dug up a massive hole directly behind the Reine compound for the installation of a new septic system. Both of those home improvements were made in the days after Wanda had gone shopping with her mother. Then there was the fact that Reine had a brother-in-law who dug graves at the historical Oak Grove Cemetery off Jones Road. During the week that Wanda vanished, there were three deaths recorded in the town of Falmouth. All three of those bodies were scheduled to be buried at Oak Grove. It is customary for grave diggers to prepare a fresh hole the night before a funeral in order to avoid disrupting a service. Investigators theorized that Reine could have asked his brother-in-law to dig one grave deeper than the others, bury Wanda and then fill in the hole with enough fresh dirt that the coffin slated for that burial spot could be placed over his wife's body. Wanda could be buried underneath any of the three elderly people who'd died in Falmouth that week, her grave marked with another name. There was even talk that Melvin had friends who poured cement for the upgraded Falmouth police station and that Wanda was part of that new construction, a rumor that persists to this day.

But by far the most grotesque theory police officers grappled with related to Melvin Reine's job in trash removal. One of the companies Reine worked for had a contract to haul scraps from local butcher shops. The crackling—tallow and fat and other animal muscle matter—would be picked up and then doused in massive vats of acidic solution to break it down. What was left was used as hand soap. Investigators knew that Melvin Reine was a very sick individual and did not rule anything out when it came to the search for Wanda's remains. No one thought that Wanda was still alive, not even her mother. And like Mary Medeiros, Captain Leonard Martin was convinced that Wanda Reine had met with foul play. Martin wanted to send Melvin Reine back to Walpole prison—this time for murder. This time for good.

Two weeks after the disappearance of Wanda Reine, Martin applied for a search warrant from the Barnstable District Court to rip up five inches of recently laid concrete in a 15-by-20-foot garage owned by Melvin Reine. The search warrant was granted and Martin thought that with it, he would be able to bring the Falmouth Fox to his knees—finally. Two days of jackhammering and thorough searches by Massachusetts State Police cadaver-searching dogs turned up nothing. The search was fruitless. Then investigators drained the murky, wet hole where the new septic system would be installed. No sign of human remains. Falmouth police even borrowed specialized high-tech laser equipment from an elite unit of the state police to search under the dirt at the cemetery. But without exhuming the bodies that had been buried there, the lasers could not locate Wanda.

Still, the search infuriated Reine. He glared out his window as backhoes ripped up the concrete and the bevy of uniformed officers walked around his property as if they owned it. At one point he clutched a pump-action shotgun in his kitchen and remarked to his brother John, "I ought to go out there and shoot all the state troopers."

John Reine talked his brother out of assassinating police officers. Secretly, though, John was hoping that the cops would find something. "What's not to like about Wanda?" he'd told investigators. "Wanda's a wonderful girl. My brother treats her like a dog, but she's a wonderful girl. I think the world of Wanda. If I could help find her, believe me, I would."

Then he let it drop: "Shirley probably knows something."

When investigators pressed him, John Reine clammed up.

The tragic fact was that Wanda's body could be anywhere, and if Shirley Souza knew something, she was not telling the police. The Reines had miles of marshland behind the compound, and owned a dump. Melvin also had access to the town dump, which had had a strange and unexplained fire in the middle of the night before Melvin Reine reported his wife missing. The craggy saltwater river near the Reine compound fed right into the Atlantic Ocean, and her body could have been swept out to sea. There are miles and miles of coastline from Woods Hole to Reine's Corner that feed into the Cape Cod Canal. Even if Martin had unlimited access to search warrants—which he did not, as the Barnstable District Court pointed out that there was no hard evidence to suggest that Wanda Reine had met with violence—the ground he would have to cover seemed limitless. He needed a blood spatter, or a confession from Melvin Reine. An article of Wanda's clothing that was described to him by her mother could have helped. But investigators had nothing, and the investigation went nowhere. In the end, Martin had to stop himself from hammering his fist into Melvin Reine's smug smile when police were forced to call off the search and pull off the Reine property.

"I told ya, Captain," Reine said through a smirk. "The cops keep driving by her. She's not missing. She just doesn't want to be found."

Reine knew that it was unlikely that the case would go

much further. He had already run into Falmouth Police Chief John Ferreira at a town gas station and issued a warning: "You want it to get hot again? This time it will be your house instead of your car."

The threat was witnessed by Melvin's brother John. He was astonished that Melvin had wagged his finger at the police chief and screamed from such a short distance that his spittle flew onto Ferreira's face.

The head of the New England organized crime family was a man named Raymond Salvatore Loredo Patriarca Sr. The reputed mob boss ran Boston's rackets from his hometown of Providence and reported the family's take to higher-ups in the Genovese crime family of New York City. He had also been at Walpole prison when Reine served time there. Melvin had boasted to his brother about befriending Mafiosi in jail—a group that John Reine wanted nothing to do with. John had started to keep his distance from his brother upon his return from Walpole.

"Melvin was always a malicious guy, but he came out of Walpole a changed man," John Reine told friends. "Now he has taken up with Shirley and he's even worse. He's got everyone in town scared of him."

Everyone but Captain Leonard Martin. Martin wanted to bring the Falmouth Fox to his knees. He did not want to give up the search for Wanda. But it is the nature of homicide investigative work that there is always another victim. Not long after leads in the Wanda Reine missing persons case dried up, Martin was promoted. He spent a brief time as the chief in Falmouth before moving on to a larger police department. Wanda's brother, Roman "Skippy" Medeiros, would become a Falmouth cop, as expected, upon his return from a stint serving in the military. He tried to keep his sister's case alive for his mother's sake. It made him sick that his mother still walked the woods around the Reine compound in hopes that she could find something of Wanda so she could at least give her daughter a proper Catholic burial. That was a prayer that Mary Medeiros offered up to her God that was not meant to be answered.

To this day, Wanda Reine's body has never been recovered; the mystery of how she vanished never unraveled.

By April of 1971, Shirley Souza was no longer just the household help. She had become Melvin Reine's lover, moving all of her belongings into the bedroom once occupied by the missing woman. Conveniently, Melvin had waited until the babysitter turned 17 so there could be no allegations of sexual misconduct with a minor. In Massachusetts, 17 was the age of legal consent. Reine had already had a close call with a statutory rape case, and did not want to take any more chances. While Reine would deny sleeping with Shirley Souza, it was common knowledge in Falmouth that she had replaced Wanda Reine as her children's mother and their father's wife.

In December of 1997, Melvin Reine filed for divorce with the Commonwealth of Massachusetts, citing "utter desertion." The complaint filed with the Probate and Family Court Department, three days before Christmas, read:

"Melvin J. Reine," Plaintiff.
  "Wanda J. Reine," Defendant.
  Plaintiff, who resides at 657 East Falmouth Highway, was lawfully married to the defendant who now resides at "address unknown." The parties were married at Dartmouth on October 26, 1964 and last lived together at E. Falmouth, Massachusetts on March 1971.

The complaint for divorce was filed when Todd and Melvin Jr. were adults, so no minor children had to be listed on the paperwork. Melvin accused Wanda of abandoning him and their children in the divorce complaint.

On or about March 1971, the defendant did utterly desert the plaintiff and has continued such desertion for one year prior to the commencement of this action.

He then asked the court to grant the divorce on grounds of "Utter Desertion."

The following day, a deputy sheriff named John S. Elliot rang the doorbell at 657 East Falmouth Highway in an attempt to deliver the divorce proceedings to Wanda Reine. The deputy sheriff did not find her and wrote:

> I hereby certify and return that on 12/23/97 I made a Diligent Search for the within named Wanda J. Reine. I was told by Shirley Souza, office manager, that Wanda J. Reine has not been seen since March, 1971.

A year after the sheriff's visit, Barnstable Family and Probate Court placed an ad in the *Cape Cod Times* notifying Wanda J. Reine that she was now a divorced woman—wherever she was. It read:

> A complaint has been presented to this Court by the Plaintiff, Melvin J. Reine, seeking to dissolve the bonds of matrimony. You are required to serve upon James H. Smith Plaintiff's attorney . . . If you fail to do so, the court will proceed to the hearing and adjudication of this action. You are also required to file a copy of your answer in the office of the Register of this Court at Barnstable.

The notice did not escape the eyes of the Medeiros family. Wanda's mother considered Reine's accusation of desertion yet another slap in the face from the Falmouth Fox. Of course, Wanda Reine did not respond to the court notices, and Melvin's divorce was eventually granted.

Once again Melvin Reine convinced a lover to forgo the formality of a church wedding or even something as simple as a dinner party. He and Shirley Souza were married by a justice of the peace in the Reine compound in 1999. He did not even take her out to dinner to celebrate. Reine may not have needed Shirley to watch his children anymore, but he certainly needed her to run the burgeoning Five Star Enterprises. By then, Reine was no longer a small-time hood and a garbage man who came home reeking of trash that made other men rich. Some of the good cops believed that Reine had built up a criminal empire on the most visible thoroughfare in the town of Falmouth, just miles away from the police station. Why couldn't he take over the town's trash trade too? Why not take over routes all over southern Cape Cod?

By the time Melvin Reine married Shirley he was a very wealthy man, and he needed a strong, steady hand to run his legitimate business while he continued to engage in his illicit money-grabbing schemes and headline-grabbing crimes. Some would say that Shirley Reine was being used by her husband to maintain Five Star Enterprises—the very business that police would come to believe provided an assassin the motive to murder her roughly six years after her wedding day. But true to form, Melvin Reine had involved Shirley in enough serious violent activities that he had a hold over her. If she tried to leave him or pilfer from the business, he would turn Shirley in for the litany of crimes that he had committed with her at his side.

The way Melvin saw it, Shirley was his accomplice in two unsolved homicide cases. One of the victims was the gas-pumping high school dropout boyfriend she had on the side while she was living with him. Another was a 17-year-old who was ready to testify against Melvin Reine, which the Falmouth Fox could not allow to happen. He did not want to see the inside of Walpole prison ever again.

"Shirley was a nice person," her friend John Boyle would say. "But she was no Cinderella."

And Melvin Reine was certainly no Prince Charming.

FIVE

Charles "Jeffrey" Flanagan had been warned by his mother not to hang around with that Souza girl who lived in the Reine compound. Nothing associated with that family amounted to much good, and Verna Collins knew it all too well. She had driven by the Reine house and noted the gilded fox on the roof as a taunt to the town that the clan was a family not afraid of anything. She had heard the rumors that the babysitter who'd moved in with Melvin Reine a year earlier was doing much more than taking care of those two little boys. But just as Wanda Medeiros had been seduced by the bad boy Melvin Reine years earlier, 16-year-old Jeff Flanagan was not deterred by his mother's warnings about the shapely Shirley Souza.

"Shirley is a fox," the teen was heard telling his friends. "She is a total fox."

Flanagan was always good with his hands, and had been attending a vocational program at Lawrence High School in Falmouth to become a plumber. But he could not hack the regular high school classes, and thus became a dropout. He landed a temporary job pumping gas at a nearby gas station. It was there that he saw 18-year-old Shirley Souza for the first time and became completely smitten. Shirley had a car, a rarity for a teenage girl in 1972. Flanagan's mother was worried every time her son climbed into the passenger seat by the black-haired beauty who had already acquired a bad reputation. Before long, Flanagan quit his gas station job and was taking off with Souza every chance he got. It made his mother feel uneasy. She was sure that whatever was happening between her son and Shirley could not end well. Everyone in town gossiped that Shirley Souza was Melvin Reine's lover.

Still, Verna Collins was not prepared for the news that arrived with a Falmouth police cruiser on a chilly October afternoon in 1972. The uniformed cop climbed out of his cruiser so slowly, she initially thought something was wrong with him. But his slow pace was prompted by nothing other than an uncomfortable dread. The worst part of the job for any police officer was this one: telling a mother that her son had been found dead; murdered, in fact. The cop was in no rush to press the doorbell and face Verna Collins. He did not need to say the words. She already felt it, an emptiness, an anxiety, a frightening shortness of breath. Innately she knew her son was dead.

Charlie Flanagan had called out to his mother over a skinny shoulder the preceding night, a Saturday. He was only 16. His birthday was in a few days and he'd wanted to celebrate with his friends.

"Ma, going to movies up the Plaza," he'd said.

The door slammed. She'd heard a car squeal down her street and past the Oak Grove Cemetery that had been searched by laser-wielding police officers for Wanda Reine's body the year before. Flanagan never made it into the movie theater. As he stood with a gaggle of other local teenagers who gathered there most Saturday nights, a dark-colored Cadillac pulled into the lot of the Falmouth Shopping Plaza. The driver pointed at Flanagan and curled his finger to gesture the teen over to the idling truck. Shirley was in the passenger seat. She looked frightened.

"I need to talk to you," the driver said. "Come here for a minute. Let's take a ride."

Flanagan opened the door of the sprawling Cadillac, hoisted himself into the passenger seat and the vehicle sped off.

Police would question Flanagan's friends. They described the mysterious driver who'd called him over as a small man with dark messy hair and "weird eyes." One of the teens was shown a picture of Melvin Reine—a police mug shot taken after his arrest for the arson spree.

"That looks like him," the teenager told investigators. It certainly made sense, considering the location of the murder scene and the method used to take Flanagan out.

His body was found on October 8, 1972, in the cranberry bog directly across the street from Reine's home by two little boys playing on the banks. The corpse was floating among the berries three feet off the pond's shoreline. The boys ran and screamed for help and yet another crime scene was set on Reine's Corner. Flanagan's body was curled in the fetal position, his hands wrapped around his calves. His small frame was bloated with the water and the weight of it gave his skin a waxy texture. It was as if someone had thrown a mannequin into the cranberry bog, the scene was so surreal.

A medical examiner would discern that Flanagan had been forced to his knees. His clothes would show dirt stains as if someone had shoved him to the cold, hard ground. There were no defensive wounds on his hands. It was as if he hadn't had the chance to fight or even beg for his life. A medical examiner would rule that Charles Flanagan's executioner had pumped a single shotgun blast into his face while standing above him. Flanagan had looked up and in that instant, the slug was fired at point-blank range. The sheer power of the blast ripped off Flanagan's right cheek and then exited out his back, leading the medical examiner to initially believe that the victim had been shot twice. That theory was wrong: The single shot was enough. Flanagan was a skinny teenager. A pellet fired from a 20-gauge shotgun by someone who'd towered over him as he knelt had created a trajectory that went through his face and out the lower base of his neck. The ferocity of the shot severed the teen's spine. The Falmouth police officers who'd responded to the scene recognized Charles Flanagan. He was a small-time hood, one of those troubled teenagers raised by a single mom in town, who had had minor run-ins with the law.

As detectives scoured the scene, Falmouth Officer Paul Poulos looked across the street at the fox glinting in the sun atop Melvin Reine's house. He shook his head sadly. It was not all that mysterious to imagine who had killed Charles Flanagan. After all, the body had been found across the street from the Reine compound. Flanagan had been spotted in Shirley Reine's car. Who else in town could be so brazen?

By then, Falmouth police officers had picked up intelligence that Melvin Reine had grown even more savage and brutal in his threats upon his return from prison. He was often heard snarling, "I'll drop a dime on you," which implied that he would hire someone to commit a shooting. More important, at least as it related to the Charles Flanagan homicide, Reine was also fond of a particular boast. It was a lesson he'd taught his young sons and a reminder that he would recite to his brother John: "Shotguns don't leave ballistics." It was true. While most firearms have a firing pin that strikes the back of a bullet and leaves a distinct marking, or a tattoo, making it easy for a forensic scientist to link a spent round to a gun, the only ballistic evidence left at the scene of a shotgun shooting are the spent cartridges—which are a dime a dozen and hard to link to a particular weapon.

Of course, that would be the case with the cartridges recovered by police officers in the scrubby dirt a short distance from the cranberry bog. The spent cartridges were untraceable. There were also the drag marks across the dirt. Flanagan had been shot dead, then dragged to the edge of the pond and dumped in. It had to have happened under the cover of darkness, detectives deduced, because of the close proximity to the road.

"Someone must have really had a deep hatred for this kid," the medical examiner, Dr. John Lewis, remarked to the homicide investigators as he examined the body. "These shots were fired at close-point range. The shotgun was held right up to his face and ripped through his back." It was clearly a crime of passion, the medical examiner asserted.

Melvin Reine may have been sleeping with women all over Falmouth, but it was Shirley he felt passionate about.

Flanagan's mother had no doubt who had hatred for her son. She knew Charlie had given Shirley his class ring, and that Shirley had been in the car the night Melvin picked up Charlie at the mall. The only man who had that kind of murderous hatred was Melvin Reine, Flanagan believed. In fact, Shirley Souza had had the gall to call Flanagan's mother days after her young friend's body was found to express her condolences. By then, Collins had already heard that Shirley had been spotted scrubbing Melvin's Cadillac in the garage behind the Reine compound. Why would Shirley Souza clean and detail the car the very day Collins' son's body was found? It was a question that Shirley Souza would never be forced to answer.

"You have a lot of balls calling here!" Collins screamed into the phone. "I know you were going with my son. I know you caused this. You wanted to make him jealous, and now my son is dead."

Shirley Souza was questioned by Falmouth police and state troopers assigned to the Cape and Islands District Attorney's Office about her relationship with Charles Flanagan. She swore that they were just friends and that Melvin did not know anything about her spending time with the swaggering teen. Melvin Reine was also questioned by the Falmouth police. He provided a weak alibi in that he'd spent the night with Shirley. As was the case any time Reine was on the periphery of a crime in Falmouth, the investigation would not go very far. Even when it appeared that the last person Charles Flanagan had been seen with alive was an older man who had summoned the teen to his car in the parking lot of the Falmouth Shopping Plaza. An older man who'd looked a lot like Melvin Reine. A man who had been driving a dark-colored Cadillac that looked a lot like the one that Melvin Reine drove, the same car that Shirley had been spotted cleaning.

But it would seem that the Falmouth Fox had struck

again. He was never charged with the murder of Charles Flanagan. Reine even had the nerve to drop by Verna Collins' house to express his condolences for her loss. She screamed at him to "get the fuck out" of her house.

It would take more than thirty years for police to develop a lead that would make it virtually impossible for anyone to argue that Melvin Reine was not involved in Jeff Flanagan's murder. That homicide was ticked off as one of the many unexplained crimes that John Reine told police he had watched his brother commit without any ramifications what-soever. John Reine knew that Melvin had wanted the teen dead. He had even watched Shirley wipe down his brother's Cadillac with a bucket, bleach and soapy water. It struck him as odd, because the Reine boys were responsible for keeping the cars clean, and Shirley was usually inside the house. Even thirty years later, John Reine remembered watching Shirley with tears in her eyes wash the inside of the Cadillac.

But by the time John spoke out in 2003, it was too late.

SIX

Paul Alwardt was one of those teenagers doomed to be labeled a troublemaker. Even as a little boy he was one of those children who tortured pets and bullied neighborhood kids, at least the ones younger than he was. Otherwise, he was usually the target of threats and taunts. After all, his looks alone would invite torment.

He had two top rows of teeth that overlapped tightly. A good dentist probably could have rectified the deformity, but his mother never took him to a good dentist. As a result his face had a malformed, frightening look. He was slight and skinny. And within days of his birth on February 2, 1960, his father Paul J., became a single parent. There is no mention of Alwardt's mother on any of the voluminous court records acquired in his short life. If anything she was a sporadic presence, primarily because she and "her people," as Cape Cod natives usually referred to the relatives of a dysfunctional family, hailed from Oak Bluffs on Martha's Vineyard. When a Cape Codder talked about someone's "people" they usually meant that the extended family was somewhat notorious, whether for alcoholic behavior or petty crime.

In the summer months, the scene at Oak Bluffs is extraordinary. Restaurants are bustling with clientele that could include pop singers, movie stars, politicians—even presidents.

Oak Bluffs in the winter months is decidedly less glamorous. The laborers who haul the island's trash and wash dishes and pump gas and babysit children are usually clustered in smaller, more dilapidated homes in that section of the island. If there was a poor section of town on an island where there are very few homes that sell for under a million dollars, Oak Bluffs would be it. Some of the laborers rent out the abandoned beach homes of summer people. Others were born into families that had for generations whaled off Oak Bluffs, used the proceeds to build humble shacks and never left. Those homes were passed down for generations and those families could not be forced out by even the craftiest of real estate agents. The Alwardts were one of those families. Hardly wealthy, they were still part of Martha's Vineyard. Their home was no waterfront retreat, but it served them well even in the long, isolating months of winter, the time of year when some families were decimated by the alcoholism that afflicted a large number of people who called the island home year round. Paul J. Alwardt took the ferry from Oak Bluffs to Falmouth—a trip that takes less than an hour—and he did not come back. At his side was his son Paul. Paul never talked about his mother much after that, police officers remembered later. Most cops thought he never saw her again.

Alwardt did the best he could as a single dad with his own issues. It did not take long for his son to look for attention in unhealthy ways—by getting in trouble. Before he was a teenager, Paul Alwardt had earned a reputation with the Falmouth police as a menace known for destruction of property and disturbing the peace. His behavior became criminal by the time he was 14. That's when he marked his first serious entry on what would become a long rap sheet. Five months after his 14th birthday, Paul Alwardt was arrested for larceny after he'd broken into a neighbor's home. His father had had enough. He petitioned the court for a CHINS warrant—Child in Need of Services—which gave a judge the authority to order local police to scoop up Alwardt and force him to show up at a supervised program after school and on weekends. In Alwardt's case, there was a program for young aspiring thugs at a YMCA youth facility in the hardscrabble city of Brockton, roughly thirty minutes away from Falmouth. Alwardt's father was grateful when police sent him there, but frankly, even he became discouraged when the scared-straight tactics at the YMCA didn't work. Paul Alwardt continued to get into trouble.

When he was 16, Alwardt was arrested for disorderly conduct. Now he had a probation officer. There was a series of petty crimes such as trespassing and graffiti. Alwardt also caught a lot of breaks from the law because both the cops and the courts felt sorry for him. He was a young kid with virtually no family. It was a classic story with many of the young toughs in town: they would do anything to get someone to look at them, notice them; it was worth taking an arrest if it meant that they would get some attention. Of course, there was only so much a judge could take, even if he recognized that Alwardt had grown up in a dysfunctional home without the benefit of the watchful eyes of a two-parent family. The small-time petty arrests would culminate with the courts sending Alwardt to a Department of Youth Services facility for delinquents. It was there, living among other maniacs whom Paul Alwardt felt he had to one-up, that his life really spiraled out of control.

He was arrested for a hit-and-run accident in a stolen car. He was arrested for throwing a brick through the window of a storefront. Then he was charged with larceny and breaking and entering. There was the day he called in a bomb hoax at the high school. He also broke into a summer cottage at night, making the home invasion a felony. He was a master at breaking into things—and out of them. One Thanksgiving, Alwardt had been locked up in the Falmouth police jail cell after an arrest for possession of burglary tools. He was in the cell alone and the station was largely deserted because of the holiday. Then–Falmouth Police Officer Rick Smith was watching a football game upstairs after checking on the prisoner. He felt someone sit down next to him. It was Alwardt.

"What the hell are you doing?" Smith bellowed. "How'd you get up here?"

"I picked the lock," Alwardt told him with a smile. Alwardt had a recognizable grin because of those two rows of teeth on his upper jaw, an abnormality that made him look a bit like a horse, Smith thought. "I just want to sit up here and watch the game with you. I won't be any trouble."

Of course, Smith escorted Alwardt back into the cell and secured the door with a set of handcuffs. But inwardly, he felt bad for Alwardt. The teen could have run out of the police station, but instead had just wanted the company of a man like Rick Smith. Smith knew Alwardt had not experienced a good childhood. Teens like him were easy prey for bullies. And Rick Smith had heard the scuttlebutt that Alwardt had been seen socializing with Melvin Reine. He knew Reine had offered the troubled teen a job at his trash hauling company. Smith was also aware that criminals like Reine knew exactly how to manipulate kids like Alwardt. A young kid would not face serious time if he were to be arrested pulling off a job—like striking a match—on Reine's behalf. Troubled kids like Alwardt were so desperate for approval it was unlikely that they would finger Reine as the mastermind of the arson. Alwardt might proudly step up and confess, maybe spend a brief stint in a juvenile detention center, and come out a hero in Reine's eyes. So Reine thought.

Alwardt was the type of kid who was grateful to make a few bucks working at Five Star Enterprises for Reine, but he was really after the accolades the older man bestowed on him. The attention from the town gangster, the infamous Falmouth Fox, meant much more to Paul Alwardt than the money.

"He was an itch. He was a pain the ass. But there was something I liked about the kid," Smith would say of Alwardt. "The kid had A.D.D., but back then they weren't giving out Ritalin or treating kids. . . . He was just a kid with a lot of problems. He didn't have it easy, and we knew it. There were a lot of cases dismissed by the Commonwealth because of the compassion rule."

As he'd done many times before with teenagers headed down the wrong path, Smith tried to lecture the teen and provide a positive influence before Reine could completely corrupt him. Unfortunately for Alwardt, it was too late.

When Alwardt's father had had enough of the mid-morning phone calls from the Falmouth police and could not afford to bail his son out of trouble anymore, he threw him out. Alwardt needed a place to stay and Melvin Reine was happy to accommodate. That way he could put the teenager to work. The first order of business was Reine's favorite: setting a fire.

On the night of April 12, 1972, Falmouth arson investigators were called to two separate fires on Paola Drive, an upscale street where waterfront cottages can rent to summer visitors for thousands of dollars a week. Two of those very expensive homes were up in flames. Back on the scene was Falmouth firefighter and arson investigator Chip Crocker, the man who'd worked the 1968 arson spree. The Falmouth police had their own investigator on the arson squad, a unit that was created because of Melvin Reine's 1968 firebug days. That man was Ahmed Mustafa. Mustafa happened to be a longtime friend of Melvin Reine. They had been seen socializing together on more than one occasion.

Even though it was April, snow can stay on the ground in Cape Cod until the first heat wave. Sometimes a snowstorm can even hit Falmouth well into the spring season and last until the first day that it was 80 degrees. Certainly there was not a classic Cape Cod blizzard that night, but enough snow had fallen that investigators could make out footprints. They followed the trail from Paola Drive through the woods and, surprise-surprise, emerged at the Reine compound. The footprints led right to the home of Adeline Carreiro, Melvin Reine's mother. Right outside her front door was a pair of soggy work boots. Inside was Paul Alwardt. The teen was out of breath and had peeled off clothes that reeked of smoke. The boots were just his size. The arson squad would not have to consult with the forensic scientists at the crime lab to figure out this caper.

Alwardt was arrested and charged with arson that night. But investigators did not believe he'd acted alone. Paul Alwardt had no motive for setting arson fires other than to garner a pat on the head from the Falmouth Fox. There might have been one set of footprints leading to the Reine compound, but no one investigating the dual fires thought that the convicted arsonist and firebug would miss out on an opportunity to watch the flames. Especially given the details in a report the arson squad had acquired written by a psychologist with the Massachusetts Department of Correction. The shrink had determined that Melvin Reine set fires for a variety of reasons. Initially it was revenge. But then, Reine got a special kind of pleasure watching something burn. The jailhouse psychologist theorized that Reine became sexually aroused at fire scenes and would often watch from a private location as flames licked at the side of a house before completely devouring it. That way he could masturbate in secret. *Maybe Reine was pleasuring himself right in his house, just feet away from his mother's in the compound*, one of the arson investigators remarked to another cop as he processed Paul Alwardt's arrest. It was an ugly thought, both agreed.

There was a practical reason that prompted Falmouth police officers to pull Reine's Department of Correction file in the first place. The fires on Paola Drive were eerily similar to the blazes set back in 1968 that had sent Reine to prison. The police were not the only ones who had access to the file. Chip Crocker was working the case for the Falmouth Fire Rescue Department, and requested a copy of the file from detectives working the case. Somehow Reine found out that Crocker had called the police department looking for the file. He was livid enough to have the temerity to call the fire department and complain about Crocker. And what would a conversation with Melvin Reine be if there was not a threat delivered? Of course Reine promised Crocker that he would be sorry. Crocker was not worried. He was not one of the Falmouth townies who allowed Melvin Reine to intimidate him.

Back at the Falmouth police station it was Officer Rick Smith who sat with Paul Alwardt. He had a relationship with the kid. After a long night in the interview room, Smith was able to convince him to cooperate with investigators. Smith talked to the kid with respect, showed him some kindness. That was enough to get Alwardt to tell him that it was Reine who'd told him to set the fires. It was Reine who'd sent him to the hardware store for fuel oil. *Sure,* Alwardt told the cop, *I'll testify against him.*

"He set me up. I'm not taking the rap for Melvin," Alwardt said. "He watched them burn."

With that, everyone agreed that Alwardt should get out of town, stay with his mother's people at Oak Bluffs. That night, the only people in the room privy to Alwardt's cooperation agreement were Rick Smith, Ahmed Mustafa, Chris Crocker and Paul Carreiro. All of the men present agreed that the arrangements would remain secret. Suspicion would later come to fall on Mustafa after he sold Reine his car. Mustafa has refused to cooperate with police or reporters. The following morning Carreiro—a longtime juvenile officer who was one of the cops who tried to mentor Alwardt— drove the teen to Woods Hole and put him on the first ferry to Martha's Vineyard.

Carreiro was a solid cop, and no one suspected that he'd leaked any information to Reine. In fact, Carreiro was one of the few local police officers who stood up to the Falmouth Fox. There were a handful of crusaders against Reine and— in their estimation—the cowards they worked alongside on the Falmouth force. Carreiro, together with Smith and Michael Mangum, had seen enough ineptitude when it came to holding the Reines accountable for their atrocities. They were a stalwart crew and would not be intimidated.

The ferry ride to Martha's Vineyard usually took less than an hour. Relatives on the island waited for the teen for three hours, but he never disembarked from any of the ferries that docked at Oak Bluffs.

Paul Alwardt was never seen or heard from again.

It's an awful feeling for a cop when he cannot trust his comrades. Everyone knew that one of the police officers in the room on the night Alwardt had agreed to cooperate must have provided information to someone who'd made the kid disappear. It was no secret that some of the cops present had long suspected that Melvin Reine was behind the murder of Charles Flanagan, a murder that was unsolved at the time of

Alwardt's disappearance (and remains a cold case even today). Investigators would later surmise that someone must have waited for Alwardt on the crowded ferry. Someone could have pulled him into the trunk of one of the cars on the lower deck. It would not have taken very much effort to heave him off the side of the boat and into the propellers of the massive ship. He could have simply been pushed into the dark open waters of the Atlantic Ocean and drowned. There were many possibilities to consider when contemplating what happened to Paul Alwardt. The list of suspects, however, was much smaller. In fact, Falmouth investigators could only come up with one name: Melvin Reine.

Alwardt's father, Paul J., who was estranged from his son at the time of the disappearance, told the *Cape Cod Times* he did not know why his son had disappeared. He did get a call from Falmouth police detectives and state police assigned to the Cape and Islands District Attorney's Office to see if he had heard from Paul. He had not. To this day, he says, he has no idea what happened to his son. He did however say that police told him they believed it was Melvin Reine Sr. who "did him in"—but with no body, there was nothing they could do.

"I feel bad, because if the kid's dead, which I assume he is, he's like a dog. It's like, 'So what?'" his father told the *Cape Cod Times* from his Nevada home. "I don't know where his body is. I feel bad that he's never gotten any justice."

There were some cops who felt the same way. This kid had had no one. In fact, he'd considered the cops who locked him up over and over again, police officers like Carreiro, the juvenile cop who drove him to the ferry, and old-timers like Rick Smith, to be friends of sorts. After Alwardt vanished, the Falmouth police force became divided. There were the stalwart supporters of Melvin Reine, fellow Cape Verdean officers who maintained a certain loyalty to their countryman. Others were simply afraid of the Falmouth Fox and steered clear of trouble with him. But after Alwardt did not make it to court to testify against Reine—and perhaps put the Falmouth Fox back into Walpole, this time for a bit longer than a year and a half—there was a group of disgusted cops who'd had enough.

They were the crusaders. They were the cops who wrote Melvin Reine moving violation tickets, pulled over his kids and wrote reports outlining reputed corruption on the Falmouth police force and presented it to town selectmen. Sadly, none of it mattered. In fact, the unspoken mission that the crusaders launched against the Falmouth Fox almost left one of their own dead on what was supposed to be another night breaking up loud and drunken holiday parties.

Certainly, John Busby thought Labor Day weekend of 1979 would be no different from any other in his career—long, busy, but financially lucrative with overtime pay. He had no idea that this year his life would be changed forever.

SEVEN

John Busby had a reputation on the streets of Falmouth. A hulking former military man who kept in shape running the rural roads and the sandy shoreline around town, Busby was called in as muscle when fellow officers wrestled with an "EDP"—an emotionally disturbed person—or needed to subdue a violent prisoner. Disorderly teens steered clear of him. Busby was well-known around the town, especially given that he had an unusual habit of wearing a helmet with a face shield to work. He also pulled on black leather gloves with knuckles lined in lead before he started each shift. Busby completed his ensemble with an extra-long nightstick that teenagers had dubbed "the Punisher." Busby had a different name for his twenty-inch baton with its six-inch handle—he referred to it as "the Prosecutor." Busby and his nightstick had become notorious in Falmouth.

It didn't help his reputation that Busby wore full riot gear even on the hottest of summer days. Most police officers wore that kind of heavy armor only when entering a dangerous situation, such as during the execution of a search warrant for a savage armed criminal or entering a drug den run by gun-toting gang members. In the military, Busby had been trained to always be ready to activate himself, so that is exactly how he dressed and behaved—like a man who was ready for action any time, any place. His gruff attitude and the strange attire prompted some of his fellow officers to grumble that he looked like he was working a war-torn area of Fallujah, when he was charged with the decidedly less dangerous job of trying to keep the summer people from getting into trouble in Falmouth and making sure drunks didn't mow anyone down on Route 28.

It also did not help Busby with some of his fellow officers that he was a by-the-book guy, the type of cop who didn't have a problem issuing the wife of an officer from a neighboring town a speeding ticket, an unspoken no-no among people "on the job" as most cops referred to themselves. Busby was not concerned about being popular. He wanted to be a good policeman.

He also wanted to be one of the crusaders against legendary gangster Melvin Reine. Within months of joining the force, Busby had noted the unimaginable pull Reine had with the top brass in the police department and the breaks that he seemed to get every time he got in trouble. It sickened Busby—so he decided that he would make it his mission to let Melvin Reine know that the act had grown tired and it would not work with at least one cop.

Busby would go out of his way to bust Reine's balls every chance he got, usually by going after lawbreaking Reine relatives.

The publicly waged war between Busby and Reine began in 1972. Busby had spent his first two years on the job hearing stories about the Falmouth Fox, the legendary racketeer who somehow managed to terrorize an entire town and its police. So he was surprised the first time he laid eyes on Melvin Reine and realized he was a small, dirty little man who looked more like a garden gnome than a truly formidable criminal. That run-in came after Busby had issued a citation to Melvin Reine's nephew for speeding around a Stop & Shop parking lot in a hot rod.

"You sure you want to do that?" the smart-mouthed kid asked Busby. "You know who my uncle is?"

Within minutes Melvin Reine pulled into the lot in a garbage truck. Someone must have called him from a pay phone to alert him that police were hounding his nephew. Reine was peeved.

"Hey, cop!" Reine yelled, as Busby would later recall in

his autobiography, *The Year We Disappeared*, which he co-wrote with his daughter Cylin. In it, he described Reine as a "small, greasy-looking dude who had everyone in town scared to death. He looked like a real nobody; his ears stuck out from beneath his pomade-slicked black hair. He had a scrawny build, maybe five-foot-something, and the posture of a man twice his age."

"What are you giving him a ticket for? He didn't do anything!" Reine screeched at Busby. "You smell smoke?"

That was the first time Reine uttered his infamous quote to the police officer. Busby had his own answer. He stared directly into Reine's close-set eyes and sarcastically responded: "You're right," making a show of taking a deep inhale. "Kind of like the candles at someone's funeral?"

That would not be the last encounter between the town's toughest cop and its most notorious tough guy.

Busby knew that the Falmouth *Enterprise* had credited Melvin Reine with fathering thirty-eight children with women in the Cape Cod areas. Most of those kids were not shy about throwing their father's name around when they got into trouble—just as his nephew had in the parking lot of the Stop & Shop. And trouble seemed to follow the Reine children, whether it was Todd and Melvin Jr., the boys everyone recognized as the Falmouth Fox's offspring, or the bastard children he secretly slipped money to women around town to help support. It was the brutal arrest of one of those children that really pitted the crusading Falmouth cops against Reine and his criminal cohorts.

On May 10, 1979, it seemed everyone in New England was glued to their television sets to watch the Bruins play the Montreal Canadiens in Game 7 of the playoffs for the Stanley Cup.

Busby was one of the untold numbers of New Englanders who threw up his hands in disgust when Montreal dashed the Bruins' chance for a win that night. His shift officially started at midnight, and it was hours before that. Busby turned his attention to his police radio, and caught a Falmouth Police officer's transmission asking for assistance with a slow-speed police chase. By the time the "chase" stopped, the cops realized that the belligerent driver who'd refused to pull over was Clyde Pena, one of the dozens of illegitimate children Melvin Reine had fathered, and one of the few he actually recognized publicly. Pena used his father's influence with abandon.

Pena had pulled his car over in a long dirt driveway on Brick Kiln Road, one of the many back roads leading toward the waterfront in Falmouth. There were four police cruisers surrounding Pena's car on the rural dirt road when Busby pulled up.

Pena had stopped the car, killed the engine, rolled up the windows and locked the doors. He refused to get out of the vehicle. Not one of the cops made a move. They were clearly confused or frightened . . . or both.

Busby looked at one of the officers and said, "Those windows are made of glass, aren't they?"

Comprehending the indirect suggestion to get physical with Reine's kid, the cop expressed a hesitant reluctance—one that Busby did not share.

"I grabbed my 'prosecutor' . . . and approached the car," Busby wrote in his autobiography.

The engine wasn't on so I knew he could hear me. I yelled, "Open up," to the guy inside. One last warning. He was a mousy dude—small and thin. He wouldn't even look up at me, so I made a quick jab at the glass with the stick, and the driver's-side window shattered. As I reached for the lock button inside, the driver reached forward and started the car, quickly putting it in gear. I wrapped my arm around him, trying to reach over to pull the key out of the ignition, but I couldn't get it.

Pena instead started the car and tried to pull out with Busby hanging on. Busby and fellow cops said that Pena dragged him, going about thirty miles an hour down Route 28. Now it was a high-speed chase.

Busby had been tossed to the ground when Pena peeled off. He got up, staggered a bit and then jumped back into his cruiser to hear a dispatcher broadcast Pena's location. Busby did not have to look up the address to know it was the Reine compound.

Where else would a Reine kid run to with cops in hot pursuit? By the time Busby pulled up, Reine was already at the door wielding a baseball bat. Pena was still in his car. He had tied his belt to a stick shift so the cops could not pull him out. Windows up. Doors locked. Uncooperative.

"That's my boy. You better not hurt him. I'll get a shot-gun!" Reine screeched at the cops. The officers took cover behind their cruisers with their guns drawn. Busby didn't. He instead pulled out his nightstick and walked up to Pena's vehicle. He smashed the window on the passenger side, opened the door, climbed in and snatched the keys from the ignition. His fellow officers were stunned.

"Busby, your head is going to be in your lap," Reine ranted. "This is not over."

Busby would recall that he responded to Reine's threats by asking him if he wanted a ride to the police station wearing shiny silver bracelets that matched his bastard son's. Another Falmouth cop trained his service weapon on Reine and told him to drop the bat. Reine reluctantly let the bat clunk to the ground. Then he wagged his finger at Busby and yelled again:

"That's my boy. You better not hurt my boy!"

Todd Reine was just a little kid that night. He was used to police being around the Reine compound, just not so many at once. There were Falmouth police cruisers and state police vehicles. It seemed that the house was surrounded by various members of law enforcement. He couldn't believe it when the biggest cop in the yard smashed the window of his half-brother's car. He couldn't believe that the cops actually pointed their guns at his father. He had never seen his father become so irate in public like that.

Todd Reine remembered the incident quite differently from the way Busby described it. He claimed that Busby smashed the windshield of Pena's car and then tried to drag him through the broken glass. When he finally wrestled Pena out of the car, Busby, Reine said, "stepped on his head with the nightstick in his neck and started to g_ind Clyde's face into the crushed stone."

An arrest log did indicate that Pena was hurt at the scene and that the "subject passed out at station/superficial injuries."

"When I got into the car with him, I was not too gentle," Busby would remember in his autobiography. "I probably stepped on him a few times."

It was the injuries to Pena that sent Melvin Reine over the edge, Todd recalled.

"Clyde weighed about a hundred and fifteen pounds soaking wet. My father came outside. He was rip-shit. He told Busby he better stop. Busby yelled back, 'You better get in the house or you'll be next!' No one talked to the old man like that. My father told the cops if they didn't get the fuck off his property, he would start his front loader and push all the cruisers into the fucking bog across the street. He meant it too," Todd Reine would say. "Those cops scattered like cockroaches when the lights go on in the room. That was it for my father. Busby was an asshole. Even the other cops on the job hated him. Busby had to go."

Pena was charged with assault and battery on a police officer, speeding, and failure to stop. The case was later dismissed because the cops had neglected to tow his car from the Reine compound, and his father had it crushed. With it went any evidence.

Melvin Reine's fury at John Busby, however, was anything but dismissed. Pena's arrest and beating established the motive Melvin Reine needed to ratchet up his long criminal rap sheet. It was a big leap from arsonist to cop killer, but some would come to believe it was a leap that Melvin Reine was willing to take, including his own brother, John.

John Reine's arrest came on a scorcher of a summer night just months after the Clyde Pena incident. He was a driver for Stop & Shop, moving food and merchandise up to stores across New England. John Reine was returning home from a run in his rig on Route 28 when he became part of dead-locked traffic. Up ahead, there had been a fatal car crash. The victim was a local district attorney named David Riley, which meant the accident brought out the big guns: prosecutors, police commanders and the Massachusetts State Police. One lane of Route 28 was closed and traffic was being inched past the police scene, around flares and orange cones set up to shield the wreckage. One car at a time was allowed to pass from either side of the thoroughfare.

Busby was directing that traffic. He stood in the street with his nightstick at his side, his bullet-proof vest zipped up tight and his riot-gear helmet on the front seat of his Falmouth police cruiser. He did take the time to pull on his lead-lined black gloves. John Reine rolled his eyes when he realized that Busby could let him pass or make him wait. The Reine compound was within walking distance and John was so aggravated by the traffic and the heat that he wanted to leap from the cab and just sprint home, leaving the rig in the middle of the highway. But he waited. And just as he'd anticipated, Busby stopped the traffic just as the truck began to maneuver its way around the orange cones.

Reine was livid. His underarms were drenched with sweat. His ass hurt from sitting all day long and he knew that John Busby was intentionally busting his balls. He waited for a full ten minutes, and with each passing second he became more agitated. Finally he couldn't take it anymore.

"Fuck Busby," John Reine said out loud to no one in particular. He gunned his engine and began to ease his truck around Busby.

Busby leapt out of the way of the behemoth of a vehicle. As it passed, he flung a clipboard at Reine's truck. He could not leave his post to give chase, especially with so many bosses around. So he wrote up a report of the incident and waited until the accident scene was completely cleared before he climbed into his cruiser and dispatched a call that he was going to the Reine compound to execute an arrest.

Busby pulled into the driveway with lights and sirens.

The commotion prompted Reine relatives to rush to their windows and pull back curtains to see what was going on. Melvin Reine went a step further. He swung open his front door and came out to the steps to scowl at Busby.

"I told you to wait!" Busby screamed as he cuffed John Reine. "You're charged with assault and battery on a police officer with a deadly weapon. You have the right to remain silent," Busby then added, automatically reciting Reine's Miranda rights.

"Hey, Busby," Melvin yelled, directly beneath the gilded fox that reminded most cops in town who he was. "Do you smell smoke?"

Busby just turned around and smiled. He was not afraid of the Falmouth Fox.

But he should have been.

Both Todd and his older brother Melvin remembered all the nights their father had vowed to take John Busby down. The first threats had come after Busby wrote the traffic ticket to his nephew. Then Reine watched the cops grind his kid's face in the dirt—on his own property. That crossed a line for the Falmouth Fox. But when his brother John was arrested, Melvin Reine snapped and swore up and down that he was going to "wipe Busby off the map." It was a promise Reine reiterated every chance he got.

The court date for John Reine's criminal case was in mid-September 1979. John Reine could not afford a conviction on an assault charge. He would lose his license to operate heavy equipment, and therefore his job. Together, the brothers hatched a plan that would prevent the case from ever going to trial.

"See, everyone thought Busby was an asshole, even his friends on the job," John Reine would later say. "I didn't think Melvin would go as far as he did."

EIGHT

Labor Day weekend is a chaotic time on Cape Cod. Swarms of tourists from Boston and New York and those cities' surrounding suburbs crowd the beaches. Restaurants are packed. Traffic is horrendous. Some locals are so grateful that the summer season is over, they'll drape sheets with the words "GOOD RIDDANCE" spray-painted on them from the overpasses lining Route 6.

Of course, the residents who taunted the vacationers who fed the tourism industry were not the ones who ran trinket shops and ice cream stores that depended on the income summer people generate from Memorial Day to Labor Day. Still, even the business owners allowed themselves a collective sigh of relief.

Fall is viewed by many as the nicest time of the year on the Cape because the crowds thin out; the weather is crisp and the restaurants are not as busy. But as the summer comes to an end every season, there is a frenzied need for folks to have one last boozy party. Of course, the combination of alcohol and the sun could always culminate into barroom brawls or road rage incidents. Every Labor Day brought an uptick in overall mayhem for the Falmouth police force.

Officer John Busby was one of the cops called in for the midnight shift on August 31, 1979. He would have loved to have had the night off, but the brass would never go for it. He was a full-timer, unlike the special summer officers they brought in and paid for part-time work. It was "All hands on deck" for the Falmouth police force on big summer holidays. Busby was just the type of cop they needed on a busy weekend, too. He was no-nonsense. The troublemaking locals were afraid of him. And even the out-of-town law-enforcement types who crowded into the area for the weekend, the city cops who wouldn't think twice about causing some trouble and "tinning" the responding officers—flashing their badges to get themselves out of a jam—respected Busby and would think twice before starting a barroom donnybrook.

That last Friday in August 1979 was a hot one, and Busby slept fitfully. Air-conditioning was a luxury that many people on the Cape did not invest in. Nine months out of the year, the Cape was cold. Even in the summer, the temperatures usually dipped enough at night that sweaty sheets were an anomaly. The problem for Busby was that when he was working the midnight shift, the only time he could catch some sleep was during the day, which could often be sweltering. Certainly, as he tried to rest before the busy Labor Day overnight, the heat was distracting him from a deep sleep. He had worked all day, wasted hours in a courtroom on a traffic violation, and now he had to try to force himself to sleep so he could be ready for the big night. As he made that attempt, Busby's wife and three children worked to paint his dilapidated Volkswagen Bug green as a surprise— a job that Cylin Busby described in the autobiography she would write with her dad decades later. Cylin and her two brothers dipped paintbrushes in leftover green paint and the result was comical. They were halfway through with the job when Busby woke up, showered and climbed inside his car— now painted headache green—for the drive on Sandwich Road to downtown Falmouth where police headquarters was located. As usual, Busby planned to be early for roll call.

As Busby drove on the dark unlit stretch of Sandwich Road past the church parking lot near his house, he did not notice the dark blue Ford station wagon sided with wood paneling, the lights off, engine running.

If he had, John Reine claims Busby would have immediately noted that he was behind the wheel. Next to him was

Shirley Souza. The one passenger Busby would not have seen was Melvin Reine. He was lying in the back seat with a pump-action shotgun cradled between his legs.

John Reine would later claim that he had been lured into the job as wheelman, that his brother had told him they were taking a ride. In fact, he would describe the night of John Busby's shooting in startling detail to Falmouth police officers more than two decades after the cop was maimed for life. The story started with Melvin Reine stomping up to John to make an announcement. It was not a question or a request. It was an order.

"I need you to drive me."

John Reine told the police he was leery that night. There was no telling what a ride with Melvin could entail. Then again, there was no such thing as saying no to Melvin. Anyone who tried was met with a scowl or a threat—or worse. Even his own brother was a little afraid of the Falmouth Fox. That made it impossible for John to ask his brother questions about the drive, like where they were going, he claimed.

So instead, John recounted, he began to walk toward the wood-paneled station wagon that had just appeared in Melvin Reine's driveway, one of the many vehicles that would only appear on the compound for a matter of days before it was crushed. That particular car had been purchased from a Falmouth police officer, Ahmed Mustafa—the same Ahmed Mustafa who was assigned to the Falmouth arson squad that had investigated Melvin Reine for the charges that had led Paul Alwardt to disappear.

"Just get in the car," Melvin said. "I'll be right back."

Melvin then went back into his own house, where his wife Shirley was cooking a quick pasta dinner for Todd and Melvin Jr. He pulled both boys aside and laid out a set of instructions aimed at his oldest.

"Melly, I want you to sit right here and listen to the police scanner. I want you to be able to tell me everything you hear on this scanner. Got it?"

Melly just nodded. His brother Todd scowled. He hated being left out, but did not dare say that to his father.

"Don't forget, Melly. I want to know everything you hear, what the police say. Write it down on this pad. Everything," Melvin yelled as he went outside to join his brother. "Shirley, let's go."

With that, Melvin and Shirley climbed into the station wagon.

"Whose car is this?" John Reine asked, as Melvin slid into the back seat. Shirley wordlessly opened the passenger-side door and sat next to John.

"It's that cop's, Mustafa," Melvin responded. "He was selling, I was buying."

Then Melvin lay down on the back seat.

"Why you sitting back there?" John then asked him.

"Don't worry about it," Melvin snarled. "Drive down Sandwich Road. We are looking for a car with a light missing. I took care of the light, smashed the light out of a car."

Melvin directed John into the church parking lot next to Busby's house. It provided cover from other passing motorists and a direct view of Busby's driveway.

"What are we doing here?" John Reine asked hesitantly. Shirley had not said a single word all night, and was not about to start speaking now. After a short, uncomfortable silence, Melvin muttered:

"You'll see."

"What car we looking for?" John asked. Melvin ignored him. The three sat in the car in an awkward silence until John asked again, "What's the car we're looking for?"

"Busby's Volkswagen. The left taillight. I took out the taillight last night so we could see the car," Melvin responded. "That guy has messed with three members of my family. It's time he paid."

With that, John Reine thought back to the night he'd had that run-in with Officer John Busby. He was aware that in just two short weeks, he would be brought to trial on charges of assault and battery on a police officer with a dangerous weapon. His entire life could be ruined. He almost felt a swell of pride that Melvin was willing to take such a risk, to threaten Busby or scare him out of testifying. He hadn't enjoyed that kind of loving relationship with Melvin since they were young kids.

John Reine would later insist that he'd had no idea that Melvin's plan was much more than a threat or a scare tactic.

John Busby had no way of knowing as he made his way down Sandwich Road that it was his own colleagues who had sold him out. A dirty cop, maybe more than one, had told Melvin Reine exactly what route Busby took to work, what time he left, and when his shift started. Another cop suspected of helping Reine was a Falmouth police officer named Arthur Monteiro, who was known around town as "Monty." Cops often joked that Monty was such a lazy police officer that he still carried the summons book he was issued in the Police Academy. Then there was Michael Leighton, suspected of being the Falmouth cop who provided Reine with Busby's schedule. The crusaders told state police that their colleague had been heard talking about Busby, and Leighton was given a lie detector test—which he failed. He was never charged, and continued to deny any involvement. Clearly the deck was stacked against Busby when his own brothers in blue were cooperating with the man who wanted him dead.

Busby was always prepared for the worst, but that Friday into Saturday morning the worst he was expecting was a few encounters with drunken knuckleheads. Ordinary summertime hijinks from amped-up college kids or out-of-control city punks from Boston neighborhoods like Southie and Dorchester.

Busby had rolled down his window to air out the stench of the paint fumes when he heard glass shatter. Suddenly it felt as if someone had set fire to his face. Two shotgun blasts exploded through the window and door on the driver's side of the Volkswagen. A third hurtled through the windshield, ripping Busby's face apart like a boot forced through a watermelon. His neck was gushing blood. His first thought was that he could not believe that he was going to die without confronting his killer. Then came the flashes of his wife and kids.

The rounds had been squeezed off from the back window of the station wagon by Melvin Reine, who had elevated his small frame by sitting on the hump in the back seat. John Reine later recalled that he'd glanced in the rearview mirror after the first shot and seen his brother with a hood pulled over his head. The hood had jagged cuts where Melvin's eyes peered out and made him look "like the Klan," John Reine told cops nearly thirty years after the shooting, referring to Ku Klux Klansmen in the South who wanted to shield their identities while committing atrocities against blacks. He'd always thought it was cowardly to lead a group like that and not want people to know who you were.

With the second blast from the back seat, John Reine looked in the rearview mirror and saw that the swift motion "twisted the hood a bit" and obstructed Melvin's view of his target.

Busby's car had begun to career off the road when the third blast shattered the window, and missed its target entirely.

"If the hood didn't get all twisted, Busby would be dead," John said. "Melvin was a perfect shot."

Sandwich Road resident Albert Santiago was watching television with his family when he heard the three explosions pop off as if cannons had been shot from Martha's Vineyard or Nantucket. He even contemplated whether a series of bombs had been set off. Then the Volkswagen Bug with the funny paint job erratically screeched into his driveway and stopped. Busby staggered out of the car, blood pouring from his face, drenching his uniform. Shards of glass were stuck in his hair and on his clothes.

"I've been shot," Busby told Santiago. "I'm a police officer."

Santiago could barely make out what the cop was saying. Busby's jaw was literally hanging from what was left of his face. He rushed Busby into his house, pressed a towel to the wound on his neck and called 911. In less than two minutes, an emergency team raced into the Santiagos' home and rushed Busby out on a stretcher. Busby was stabilized at Falmouth Hospital and then taken to Massachusetts General Hospital by ambulance.

The Reines and Shirley drove back to the compound. Melvin was boastful, puffed up and pleased with his actions. According to interviews and police officials, he went as far as to tell the story of the shooting to his young sons. By then John Reine had retreated to his own home. He was still stunned when he pulled into the compound. He turned off the ignition, handed the keys to Melvin Reine and walked into his own house and shut off the lights. He wanted to forget what happened.

That night and the plot against John Busby would mark the end of John Reine's relationship with his brother. John Reine never got a good night's sleep after that. It was not the guilt of the assassination attempt on Busby—the insomnia was provoked by John's own fear. Melvin Reine had a storied history of making anyone who could testify against him and send him back to that hellhole at Walpole disappear. John Reine was under no delusion that the bloodline he shared with Melvin would necessarily keep him safe from harm or retribution—and Melvin Reine soon came banging on the door to confirm John's fears with an implied threat.

"Don't say nothing," Melvin snarled at him, his voice menacing and low, a voice John had heard his brother use in the past to threaten police chiefs, wealthy business owners and local hoods. "Don't open your mouth. Me and Shirley won't say nothing and neither will you. Stay quiet."

Secretly, the boys would later tell their uncle, Melvin was pissed that his brother was not more appreciative. After all, he had succeeded in getting the assault case against John dismissed by a judge. Melvin Reine was also the type of man who needed to brag about any big scores that he pulled off, and the night of the Busby shooting was no different. He wanted to share a laugh with his brother, back-slap one another. But John had retreated into his own house before that could happen. No matter. Melvin Reine had an appreciative audience in his young sons, and began to tell them that Busby was dead.

Of course, that prediction was premature, but it was captivating storytelling regardless.

"At first we had to let him pass because there was another car in the area," Melvin breathlessly told the boys. "Plus, he painted the thing. I didn't see it at first. It threw us off."

As the boys stared at their father with utter adoration, an ambulance raced out of Falmouth Hospital and made its way to the best emergency room in the country at Massachusetts General in downtown Boston.

Emergency room doctors who dealt with incredible trauma every night at MGH were still startled when they saw the extent of Busby's injuries. They were desperately trying to keep the critically wounded cop alive, and needed to hook him up to a respirator to pull the shards of glass from his neck and stop the blood loss that could kill him. As a team of doctors scrambled to save his life, Busby scribbled a note to his wife, Polly.

Polly Busby, who alternated between hysterical tears and absolute fury, showed her husband's scribbles to the good guys on the job, a couple of the crusaders, Michael "Mickey" Mangum and Rick Smith. Mangum, after all, had tried to blow the whistle on corruption in the department shortly after Alwardt disappeared, but he was snubbed by the town selectmen. The same selectmen who continually gave Reine's trash-hauling company lucrative contracts even when he was caught breaking the law time and time again. Mangum did not need to read his critically wounded friend's words to know what the note said.

This was not an accident. This was intentional. Protect the kids. Melvin Reine was responsible.

NINE

Television cameras and local reporters crowded outside the emergency room at Massachusetts General Hospital. After a while, Busby's friend, Falmouth Sergeant Richard Corey, came outside to make a solemn statement to the press. Inside, Busby was being prepared for what would become a nine-hour surgery. Of course, they could never make his face fully functional. No amount of reconstruction could allow him to chew properly again. His cheeks would never be full. His smooth skin would be jagged with scars. His own children would not recognize him for well over a year. Emergency room doctors were not thinking about any of that, even if Busby's wife Polly had those thoughts in the back of her mind. Surgeons were not concerned about Busby's looks. They needed to keep him alive. To do that, doctors first had to carefully remove glass and bone fragments from his eyes and skin. The bleeding had to be staunched. They had to make sure that buckshot had not traveled into his arteries. They had to make sure that John Busby would survive that night.

Usually the mid-morning shooting of a police officer—especially one that left a cop critically wounded—brought out the town officials and the big guns of law enforcement. John Busby had watched that type of response himself when that district attorney had been killed on Route 28. The town selectmen usually came, along with the occasional state senator or representative, to shake hands with the police officers who lingered in the emergency room in a silent vigil for the critically wounded cop. That night though, there was a glaring absence of public officials as Busby fought for his life. Falmouth Police Chief John Ferreira did not bother to show up, a highly irregular move, even if the cop had been badly wounded in a traffic crash—never mind the fact that there'd been an attempt on his life. Every police commander makes an appearance at the hospital. In fact, in most cities, like New York and Boston, both the mayor and the police commissioner show up at a cop's bedside after a police shooting even if the attack took place on the morning side of midnight and they were asleep.

Ferreira would visit Polly Busby at her home, "I know how you feel. This guy set my car on fire," Ferreira had the audacity to tell her, undoubtedly thinking his words would assuage some of her anxiety. They didn't. As she would later tell her husband's friends, the crusaders, the chief really did not see a world of difference between the destruction of his personal property and the attempt on John Busby's life. It showed not just a complete lack of judgment, but also a callous attitude toward the nature of the attack against Busby. Sure, everyone knew that Busby was not a go-along-to-get-along type of guy, which meant that he made his boss' job more difficult. But Ferreira had to understand the symbolism of a police chief not bothering to pull himself out of bed to visit the family of a cop clinging to life. And he had to know that there were others watching, not the least of whom were the state police. Some of the Massachusetts troopers were completely unaware of the sway that the Falmouth Fox had in the town, and were perplexed by the police chief's absence.

Befuddlement turned to concern for the Massachusetts State Police after Ferreira rebuked their offers to help catch Busby's would-be killers.

Anytime there is a call for an officer down, police officials from all over the country volunteer to help in the hunt for the shooter. That was the reaction from Massachusetts State Police troopers who flooded into Falmouth with offers of extra manpower. Cops from surrounding Cape Cod towns volunteered to assist. Even New York City detectives vacationing in Falmouth for Labor Day weekend volunteered to act as errand boys, delivering coffee to investigators or running evidence to the state police crime lab nearly an hour away. That is the way it is when a cop is shot. That reaction does not have a jurisdiction. Everyone in law enforcement wants immediate action and swift justice for a wounded compatriot. But for some inexplicable reason Ferreira declined all offers of help from outside agencies. Because Busby had survived the shooting, barely, the state police did not have jurisdiction. Cops from other small Cape Cod towns were told to butt out. Even the vacationing NYPD detectives were told to keep sunning themselves on the sandy beaches and to let Falmouth take care of their own.

The town did seem to take particularly good care of one person: the Falmouth Fox. Only this time the bungling of the Falmouth police force was playing out across the state. There was an audience—one that had trouble grasping why a police chief would not want the shooters of his own cop captured. It did not take long until it was suggested that Chief Ferreira enjoy his retirement. Weeks after Busby's shooting, Ferreira resigned.

Still, the damage was done. No one would be arrested for Busby's shooting. There was not even a report written that the description of the would-be assassins' car closely matched the one that Falmouth Officer Ahmed Mustafa had recently gotten rid of. Sure enough, Mustafa had just sold his old wood-paneled station wagon to his buddy Melvin Reine. He apparently did not think it was worth mentioning after the Busby shooting. Mustafa didn't show up in the emergency room the night Busby was shot either. Corey took note of that. So did Rick Smith and Mickey Mangum. Mustafa continues to refuse to comment. In fact, decades later investigators and reporters would learn there were no reports to be found on the Busby case at all.

Corey still had to issue a statement to the press. It had been a long night. It still remained unclear if Busby would even survive. Corey's worry was etched into his face. He did not want to plan a cop's funeral. He certainly did not want to attend one. Especially for a friend. No one did. He thought of his own family as he looked into the banks of television cameras.

"We haven't got anything in the way of leads at this point," Corey said. "We're still banging on doors. We might not be able to come up with anything until we can talk to Busby himself.

"He is one of our best cops. Everybody liked him. He was a regular guy. A good family man. All police officers have enemies, but he didn't have any more than the rest of us."

Even as he said those words, Corey knew that it was probably not the number of Busby's enemies that had provoked the ambush—it was the type of enemy: a particularly vindictive enemy who people believe had gotten away with a lot of criminal behavior over a very long period of time.

"We've all got to be careful," Corey said to the press, but it was a comment clearly aimed at his fellow crusaders on the Falmouth police force. "No one knows what's going on. We don't know of any motive. Until we do, all of us have to watch our backs."

That is, everyone but Melvin Reine. Once again, the Falmouth Fox would not even be brought in for questioning.

Outwardly, it appeared that Falmouth rallied around the Busby family. As he recovered from the buckshot wounds that wrecked his head and face, a $5,000 reward was offered for information that could lead to the arrest of his shooters. Bills mounted as Busby spent more than a month at Massachusetts General Hospital, so fundraisers, or "times" as they are called in New England, were held in the town and were well attended. A group of runners with the Falmouth Track Club even set up a version of the nationally vaunted Falmouth Road Race that November, months after the regular annual August marathon, to benefit the Busby family. The Massachusetts Safety Officers League kicked in cash to help the father and his three kids. The Busby family was granted around-the-clock protection, which strained the police manpower budget after overtime costs reached upwards of

$30,000. The town also raided the budget to buy the Busbys a guard dog—a specially trained German shepherd named Thor. Selectmen also agreed to build an eight-foot fence around Busby's home, which gave the family the feeling of living in a bunker.

But none of it was enough to make them feel safe. By the following summer, the Busbys had packed up and moved out of Falmouth for good. Busby's sons Eric and Shawn were being taunted and harassed at school. Other little girls were not allowed to play with his daughter Cylin because their parents were afraid the Busbys all had targets on their backs. The Busbys wanted their children to grow up properly, without police details and guard dogs. They moved South and would not come back until 2005—after Shirley Reine was murdered and Busby discovered that her stepsons and her husband's brother had made statements to police that implicated the man he had suspected even as he was hooked up to a respirator:

Melvin Reine. The Falmouth Fox.

TEN

Confessions don't happen often, especially the type of heart-wrenching, detailed purging of information that John Reine provided about the night he acted as the wheelman in the attempted murder of John Busby. John Reine knew everything. He knew that his brother had bought the car used in the attempted hit on Busby from a Falmouth police officer. In fact, the Falmouth Fox was the master of having untraceable cars. He would offer to have the guys at the trash company detail the cars of friends, or even passing acquaintances. Then, if there was a fire set or a crime committed, witnesses would spot a car that was not traceable to Reine, but to some hockey mom in Falmouth, or even a priest or a fellow member of a Cape Verdean social club. The information John Reine had went well beyond intricate knowledge of the Busby hit. John Reine knew that his brother had had a grudge against Jeff Flanagan, the kid who'd been found assassinated in the cranberry bog across from the compound. John Reine also claimed that Mustafa told the Falmouth Fox that Paul Alwardt had agreed to testify, that Alwardt had provided details on materials used in the arson attacks and instructions that were given him. He even felt bad about the disappearance of Wanda Medeiros Reine and had the same suspicions everyone else did: Melvin made his wife disappear so he could sleep with the teenage babysitter.

John Reine's information was useless in the Busby investigation. It would have been enough to present to a grand jury to get an indictment—if John Reine had come forward before the statute of limitations. If he had provided information before his brother had been sentenced to rot in an insane asylum.

But John Reine was not the first to cooperate with police. He was convinced to sit down and spill his guts only after his beloved nephews had done so first. In that interview, they had given up John Reine as the getaway driver in the Busby shooting. By then, the Busbys were long gone, living in hiding. Busby's life would never be the same. Busby was a hard guy, a guy in control who protected his family and his honor above all else. It was not just his face that was disfigured, it was his pride. Old habits die hard, and Busby had acquired a masculine swagger, a tough-guy image while serving in the military. Emaciated and maimed, Busby felt like he'd lost part of his manhood—and he wanted to get it back by striking out at Melvin Reine. He knew that the Falmouth police, with the exception of the crusaders, would not even try to solve the case. As a result, every time he thought of the Reines and the cluster of lowlifes who lived on the compound, he had to choke back an acidic bile that rose in his throat. Of course he wanted revenge. It was not as if Busby never thought about Melvin Reine's body floating in a cranberry bog on Cape Cod; it was just that the maimed police officer was not willing to say goodbye to his family to do time for a creep like the Falmouth Fox.

Cape and Islands District Attorney Michael O'Keefe did not have the authority to charge John Reine in the Busby shooting because of the statute of limitations. But it did puzzle a lot of law enforcement types that he did not present evidence to a grand jury about the Flanagan homicide, a crime for which there is no statute of limitations. John Reine's information might have swayed a grand jury to indict Melvin, even if he was living in a nuthouse. At least the charge could have brought some peace of mind to Jeff Flanagan's mother. She would die without knowing who'd killed her son, or why. John Reine had some ideas though. Ideas that he was happy to present to the Falmouth Police.

"Flanagan used to come around the yard all of the time," John told police, adding that he suspected that his brother had been the one who forced Flanagan to his knees before blasting the teen with a shotgun slug. "I asked Melvin about why the police were at the bogs. Did you hear Jeff Flanagan was shot there?"

Melvin did not respond. But John Reine knew that his silence was an admission. It was one of the reasons he had been afraid of his brother for such a long time. He was sick to his stomach that day he watched Shirley, just a teenager herself, scrubbing the inside and the outside of Melvin's Cadillac hours before the police would surround the cranberry bog to investigate the body found in its murky waters. The detectives asked John Reine why Melvin would want the teenager dead.

"To send a message," John Reine responded, his voice tinged with a hit of perplexity as if the cops were stupid for even asking. The murder sent a message all right. From the time Flanagan's bloated body was fished out of the cranberry bog until Reine was committed, it did not appear that Shirley ever took up with another man besides Melvin. As far as Alwardt's disappearance, John Reine said his brother had complained that the teen had told arson investigators about a fuel oil purchase he'd made for Melvin. When investigators asked John Reine how his brother could have found out, he responded again with a bemused look.

"Simple. Mustafa told him. The kid told Mustafa about the fuel oil and about the arson that Melvin did," John Reine told investigators. "Melvin found out about it."

By then, Mustafa had retired from the police force. He was a politician now; a town selectman. He has repeatedly denied any wrongdoing. He admitted that Melvin Reine was a friend of his and yes, he'd sold him his wood-paneled station wagon back in 1979. He had explained that away to other cops, the crusaders, by saying that it was just part of growing up in a small town. So, sure, he had been friendly with Reine. But other than that, there was no impropriety. In 2008, he became a town selectman. A local blogger on www.wickedlocal.com/falmouth interviewed Mustafa about what he could bring to the table as a Falmouth leader. The interview went like this:

Ahmed Mustafa

Address: Carriage Shop Road, East Falmouth

Age: 70

Occupation: retired state police officer

Family: married with four grown daughters

Education: Master's Degree in criminal justice

Civic involvement: current selectman; life member, AMVETS, VFW, DAV; member, East Falmouth Village Association; Town Meeting member, Precinct 4.

Most important issue facing Falmouth: "Basically, for us to be able to make it to the future," says Mustafa, who spoke of the current economic times and rising prices. "I just hope we can pull it out."

What he brings to the table: "This is my hometown and I'm not going anywhere," says Mustafa. "I'm concerned about our future to make sure that everyone has a fair and just share of our community."

A great example of Falmouth's spirit is: its diversity and knowledge. "We have a diversity and a knowledge base that we haven't even begun to tap," says Mustafa. He also says the town has the ability "to work together when things get tough."

Last book read: "I've never been one who can sit down and read a book from cover to cover," says Mustafa.

But he is quick to point out that he urges his grandchildren to become avid readers. "I'm not a reader and I'm fine with that but I tell them not to do what I've done because I had to learn out in the world, the hard way."

What people don't know about Mustafa is: not much. "I actually think most people in this town know what I'm about," says Mustafa.

He says he's not really into any hobbies or collections but does love to read about new ideas, new technologies, new ways to build a better mousetrap.

"I love to go on the computer and research things," says Mustafa. He adds that, in doing so, he's following the advice of a good friend and fellow retired officer: "be amenable to new things and change with the times."

Some of the crusading cops who still resented Mustafa for not being honest about his role in the Busby shooting rolled their eyes when they read his interview, especially when he declared, "I think most people in this town know what I am about." Yes, Ahmed Mustafa, there were still cops who remembered the wood-paneled station wagon that had been used to transport Busby's would-be killer, There were cops who remembered the BOLO—Be On The Lookout—for a wood-paneled station wagon that was broadcast over every single Falmouth police radio and that Mustafa somehow thought the fact that he had just sold one to the town's gangster was not worth mentioning. They felt like they knew exactly what Mustafa was about.

Mustafa may have spent his life living in Falmouth, but his career would take a different path. After Ferreira left the force, Mustafa also left to join the Registry of Motor Vehicles Police. When that department merged with the state police in 1992, Mustafa became a trooper. He retired as a state police lieutenant. When pressed by fellow cops about Melvin Reine, the recently elected town selectman would point to his long legacy of service to his country as a member of the Air Force and then as a thirty-eight-year lawman.

Then there was "Monty"—Arthur Monteiro, the former Falmouth police officer who was a longtime friend of Melvin Reine. John told investigators that "Monty" had come by the Reine compound after Busby was shot so he could share a laugh with the Falmouth Fox. He also kept Melvin Reine abreast of any developments in the apparently nonexistent investigation. Why wouldn't he? He made plenty of money on the side to supplement his paltry police salary by doing construction work for Melvin Reine.

For some reason, those two cops were never criminally charged or even disciplined by the brass on the police force. Nor would they be called in front of a grand jury even after Melvin Jr., Todd, and John Reine gave statements to police about both Mustafa and Monteiro's involvement with the Falmouth Fox in 2003. They escaped questioning when John Reine bolstered his nephews' statements about police corruption. Nor would they be questioned two years later, after Shirley Reine was found shot dead in her home. Certainly another dead body with close ties to Melvin Reine should have at least provoked a grilling of the cops close to him. Somehow, though, it never happened.

The fact that the confession of John Reine was largely ignored angered a lot of cops, and they turned their ire toward Cape and Islands District Attorney Michael O'Keefe.

O'Keefe had been a prosecutor for a long time. He knew it would be nearly impossible to open the cold case homicide of Charles "Jeff" Flanagan. It had taken place back in the 1970s. No one was pressing police for answers now that Flanagan's mother had passed. The rest of the murders that Melvin Reine was suspected of committing had no bodies, therefore, no evidence. Trying to put someone away for murder without a body is a nightmare for prosecutors. Besides, it's difficult to pursue a murder case against a madman. So O'Keefe did not even bother to try. Instead he suppressed the police report detailing John Reine's confession. He wouldn't allow anyone to read another police report filed after Melly and Todd walked into the Falmouth police station to spill their guts about their father's role in Busby's shooting.

The boys would say that their motivation was a push to find out the truth about their mother, Wanda. Of course, most people weren't buying that sob story, and believed that the boys were largely motivated by money. They wanted to punish Shirley because they had been written out of their father's will.

Still, none of that should have mattered to the district attorney, who seemed more concerned with stopping the leaking of information than he was about finding justice for the people who'd met violent ends at the hands of Melvin Reine.

It appeared that the Falmouth Fox would escape prosecution for every one of the crimes that his brother had implicated him in, and which investigators had long suspected him for. Sure, hospital records indicated that Melvin Reine was not cognizant of right and wrong, and spent most days urinating on the beds of fellow patients at Taunton State Hospital. Some investigators mused that Reine was "crazy like a fox," and pointed to the notorious antics of reputed Genovese crime family boss Vincent "The Chin" Gigante. Gigante was an infamous New York City crime lord who, for decades, thwarted federal agents from charging him with a single crime because he wandered through his Greenwich Village neighborhood in New York City in a bathrobe, mumbling to no one in particular, crumbs adhering to his scraggly beard. Gigante's nut-ball act would keep him out of prison for decades, until he was well into his seventies, when federal prosecutors successfully argued that he had faked mental illness for years to obstruct justice. He was eventually convicted for a plethora of racketeering-related crimes and, in an attempt to shave time off his sentence, even copped to the bogus cuckoo act. The mob boss earned his nickname "The Chin" because he refused to talk out loud in case the government was listening, and would instead stroke his chin to communicate with his Mafia underlings. In the end, Gigante could not communicate with anyone. He died in a federal prison in 2005 when he was 77 years old.

Melvin Reine looked up to guys like Gigante, and bragged that he had made underworld connections while serving out his arson sentence at Walpole. It was the Genovese crime family that had branched out into Springfield, Massachusetts—a gritty city where the New York mobsters that worked for Gigante opened strip clubs and paid off politicians. It made sense that Genovese crime family gangsters would befriend a guy like Melvin Reine, who had cops in his pocket. Maybe he had chuckled over Gigante's ruse with some of his underlings at Walpole—at least that's the story that John Reine was spinning.

John Reine told police he had grown to be afraid of his brother after Melvin had been released from Walpole and begun to associate with mobsters from Boston's North End and Federal Hill in Providence. He had seen Cadillacs and Lincoln Continentals pull up to the Reine compound, and watched as his brother slipped envelopes into the open cracks of windows. Besides, Reine had outfoxed cops for so long, it was not completely unreasonable to suspect that he'd acted irrationally in a courtroom so he could avoid a trial. Besides avoiding justice, the Falmouth Fox had no reason to leave Taunton State Hospital. His own sons had turned against him, telling the police about his criminal capers. His brother had cooperated against him alongside his own sons. Shirley was dead. Who was at home for him?

Even if Melvin Reine were to suddenly feel not so crazy, there were two disappearances of people close to him that he would have to explain: the murder of his babysitter's boyfriend, and the shooting of a Falmouth police officer. What

kind of incentive did Melvin Reine have to respond to psychiatric treatment?

A soft bed in a hospital ward with nurses who, for the
most part, were easy on the eyes beats a cot in a cell with a
vicious con at Walpole any day.

ELEVEN

John Busby was a realist. He knew he could not seek revenge. If he went after Reine himself, he would be caught. He was as sure of that as he was that the Falmouth Fox had orchestrated his shooting, and had likely squeezed off the shots himself. If Busby were to pursue that selfish need to see Melvin Reine suffer and get caught and sent to prison, the toll it would take on his family would be too much. They had already seen their lives uprooted by violence. Busby also knew that Cape Cod officials were not going to be overzealous about seeking the truth, which could not make anyone in Falmouth look very good—including the Cape and Islands District Attorney.

There was nothing O'Keefe could do about the statute of limitations. Besides, there were some cops who thought that there was not a district attorney in the state who would want to open up an investigation on a case like the Busby shooting, regardless of the limitations. It would undermine law enforcement agencies across the state if it was revealed how many times the Falmouth Police Department allegedly looked the other way when it came to Melvin Reine.

O'Keefe had been a prosecutor under his mentor and predecessor Philip Rollins for decades before he was elected into the position as the top law enforcement officer on the Cape and Islands. It seemed the minute that he was sworn in in January 2002, O'Keefe's life was mired in controversy.

Within days, fashion writer Christa Worthington was raped and murdered in her wealthy family's Truro cottage, with her 2½-year-old daughter Ava at her nipple trying to nurse. The little girl had tried to revive her mother by feeding her lifeless body with sippy cup. The body was found by Worthington's former lover, a children's book illustrator named Tim Arnold who had driven to the cottage to return a flashlight and saw little Ava over her mother saying strange phrases like: "Mommy lying down. Mommy dirty. Mommy won't get up. Tried to clean Mommy."

It would take O'Keefe almost three years to announce the arrest of her killer, an ex-con who worked as a trash man and admitted to an affair with Worthington, a single mother who had retreated to the Cape after a successful writing career in New York City. The trash man's name was Christopher McCowen, a 33-year-old drifter who was convicted in 2006 on charges that he'd broken into her remote home and savagely raped, beaten and stabbed her, leaving the baby alone with her mother's lifeless body. McCowen already had a lengthy rap sheet that included a 7-year prison stint for a Florida home invasion and an arrest on charges that he had threatened to kill his daughter's mother. In fact, he had a long and ugly history of violence against women.

"Police were aware of him," O'Keefe said at a press conference announcing an arrest in the Worthington case. There were reporters there from across the country. The case had been covered heavily by the media and there were several books either in the stores or being written at the time of McCowen's bust. He then added that investigators "certainly know the motive," but declined to elaborate. O'Keefe insisted that Worthington did not appear to have known McCowen, an employee at a hauling company that removed her garbage every Thursday. "There is no evidence whatsoever to suggest there was any relationship whatsoever between them other than him walking up her driveway to collect her trash," said O'Keefe, who had suggested in the past that Worthington had been intimately involved with her killer—an assertion that earned him the ire of her family, who then demanded that he be taken off the case. But there was no one else with the knowledge of the case that O'Keefe had, and he stayed. He earned the right to stay on. O'Keefe was a well-respected district attorney in Massachusetts. In fact, he had been awarded the prosecutor of the year honor and managed the superior court and five district courts in his command well.

But O'Keefe did get a black eye from Maria Flook's unflattering portrait in *Invisible Eden*, when she described him conducting an interview wearing nothing but a towel. The book was a disaster for prosecutors. Flook, a novelist with no journalistic experience, inadvertently revealed her law enforcement sources and made it difficult for police to argue that they did not skewer some suspects in the press before they had a day in court. Flook's book was released in 2003, nearly two full years before McCowen would be arrested in April 2005. O'Keefe's credibility was in question after the book's publication because it was glaringly apparent that he had shared information with the novelist that could have tainted the investigation.

That book created a buzz, but it was nothing like the beating O'Keefe would suffer in another book written by the writer Peter Manso and slated for publication in 2009. Manso was born and raised in Manhattan, but spent summers on the Cape. As if being a New Yorker was not enough of a reason for New Englanders to despise him, Manso was also viewed as a pompous, self-promoting gadfly. His biography of Norman Mailer had earned him the moniker "poison drip" from his subject, and he'd also penned a book that infuriated the wealthy gays who settled on the very tip of Cape Cod in Provincetown. After saying that the longtime resort town attracted the country's best artists and writers, his book insinuated that Provincetown had turned into a shallow cesspool of buff boys and uptight lesbians obsessed with redecorating and arugula. But Manso's book on the Worthington case infuriated a lot of law enforcement officials and raised new questions about O'Keefe's handling of the case. Then again, Manso was unabashedly tied to McCowen's defense team and went as far as to request cross-examining a witness on the stand, which is illegal in

Massachusetts. He was a writer, a civilian, not an attorney representing a killer. It was an outlandish suggestion and one that was summarily dismissed by the judge.

To this day, Manso is convinced that McCowen was a victim of racism, and told *The Boston Globe* that the police misconduct he uncovered was so egregious he could only describe it this way: "the Cape is a suburb of redneck Mississippi." Manso pointed to the accusations that some of the jurors on the case were racist after remarks made during deliberations forced Judge Gary A. Nickerson to interview a dozen jurors about their personal beliefs about black men. Manso bought McCowen's story that his friend, Jeremy Frazier, committed the murder and said that prosecutors had quashed evidence that could have persuaded a jury of the same theory.

Before the publication of the book, Manso was arrested by Truro police on a dozen firearms charges. Manso claimed that the police targeted him for revenge after he'd pointed out their errors, as prosecutors argued that the stash of weapons—including an assault rifle—recovered from the writer's Truro home were illegal because he did not have a valid firearms license and the guns did not have the required trigger locks. Manso had heard of the unsolved murder of Shirley Reine and snickered to his attorney that Melvin Reine and his family comprised exactly the type of clan able to corrupt a police department. If the Reines could undermine law enforcement in Falmouth, what made Truro—another insular Cape Cod tourist town—any different?

After his arrest, McCowen told state police that he'd had consensual sex with Worthington, then watched as Frazier beat her to death.

"These cases are very difficult," O'Keefe said when asked if he had any regrets about suggesting that the victim had been a promiscuous woman killed by one of her many lovers. "I explained my feelings on the matter." It was an odd statement, because O'Keefe had never discussed his "feelings" with reporters. Not then, and not now.

The victim's cousin, Jan Worthington, a Truro Police

Department dispatcher who attended McCowen's arraignment and O'Keefe's press conference, said her family had begun to lose hope that Christa's murderer would be found, even with a $25,000 reward raised by her loved ones.

"It was hard to think this would come to an end," she said. "We are all relieved it was not someone close to us."

What she meant was that the family was grateful that the killer was not someone Worthington had been in love with. Before McCowen was arrested, the investigation had focused on handsome, rakish Provincetown shellfish constable Tony Jackett, a married man who'd fathered the victim's daughter, Ava. Jackett's marriage survived the media scrutiny, the revelation of the affair and even the suggestion that he was the killer. The Jacketts are involved in raising Ava, along with Worthington's close friends. Tim Arnold, the children's book illustrator who found her body, was also implicated as a potential suspect in the press after prosecutors hinted that he was being eyed. Even Worthington's own father, Christopher "Toppy" Worthington, came under scrutiny after he took up with a former heroin-addicted prostitute, Elizabeth Porter. Porter was also a known thief, resentful that her boyfriend's daughter had taken money from her wealthy dad. The suspicions and finger-pointing divided Cape Cod and became ceaseless fodder for gossip by the full-time residents. Everyone close to Worthington prayed that her killer was not one of the people in their tight-knit circle.

Until his 2005 arrest, McCowen's name had not arisen in the case, despite his criminal history and the number of times that he had been to Worthington's home. Still, McCowen's bust came as a relief to a number of people who'd spent years living among neighbors who eyed them nervously in the supermarket or at church after the district attorney suggested they could be responsible for the homicide. No matter what Peter Manso believed, those closest to Worthington were just grateful that someone had been identified, even if the case would once again expose inadequacies in the investigation run by Michael O'Keefe.

First, O'Keefe explained the delay by saying that Massachusetts State Police homicide investigators had had a tough time tracking down McCowen. Especially after it had been revealed that he was among the men who had submitted a DNA sample. He was also well-known to the state police who worked Cape Cod because he was frequently arrested for beating women.

As recently as January 2004, McCowen was arrested in Eastham after he'd told the mother of his 2-year-old daughter, Misty, that he would "snap [the mother's] neck." She obtained a restraining order barring him from her home, her job and their daughter's daycare, according to court records filed at Barnstable County Probate Court. Before that, in 1999, Wellfleet police arrested him for smashing a former girlfriend with her own car door after breaking into her apartment. He was ordered to attend counseling, but then never showed up, according to Orleans District Court records. At his arraignment in 2005 yet another woman—a robustly built bottle blonde who identified herself as McCowen's girlfriend—whispered to him from behind long pink fingernails at his arraignment.

"He's not a rapist-killer," she told reporters after she waved goodbye to McCowen in court. "He's a nice guy." But he was not a nice guy at all. Now he will serve life in prison.

Of course, the Worthington homicide was not the only high-profile murder case that O'Keefe had to grapple with. In fact, the homicide clearance rate for his office was roughly 90 percent, which meant that the state police troopers assigned to investigate homicides in his office solved most of the cases that were in front of them. One of those cases involved a murderous, thieving Roman Catholic priest and his reputedly gay lover.

Boston had still been reeling from the Catholic priest scandal on September 20, 2003, when the body of a handsome young golf pro named Jonathan Wessner was found stabbed and beaten to death on a beach not far from Woods Hole. That murder would eventually take down a 70-year-old priest from a Falmouth church, a priest who had pilfered hundreds of thousands of dollars from his parishioners and had been sleeping with the parish handyman, a convicted pedophile named Paul Nolin. That priest, Bernard Kelly, had given Nolin keys to St. Joseph's tall stone church bell tower; the spot where police said the handyman lured the golf pro with a promise of a stunning beach view. Weeks later, Wessner's partially decomposing body was found under a pile of rocks near a boat house on the beach. He had been stabbed repeatedly and bludgeoned with a blunt object. He was only 20 years old and a well-known fixture at The Woodlands golf and country club.

It did not take police long to track down Nolin. He had left his car at the rectory of St. Joseph's Church in Woods Hole, where his good friend and reputed lover Bernard Kelly was the priest. Kelly did not live in the rectory, he just worked there. After all, Kelly owned a sprawling home that was worth $3.5 million, a house that was hidden by a gate and paid for with monies that the priest had embezzled from a number of Cape Cod churches that he had served. The house even had a grandiose name, Fox Glen Morgans. The estate lived up to the fancy name. The 7,300-square-foot mansion was nestled alongside a picturesque pond and boasted an in-ground swimming pool, a stable big enough for ten horses and a six-car garage. The place would remain Kelly's secret until his good "friend" Nolin was arrested for the murder of Wessner. In fact, the case would be investigated by one of the Falmouth police force's crusaders, Rick Smith. Nolin told Smith that Wessner had arrived at his home at approximately 2 a.m.; and that many of the partygoers, including Nolin, began consuming cocaine. The coke fueled nonsensical conversation about everything from Cape Cod beaches to religion. Nolin invited Wessner to visit the bell tower in Woods Hole. They went to the tower at about 7:30 a.m. There Wessner offered Nolin cocaine, but Nolin refused because he had to work. After about ten minutes, they left in separate vehicles. Nolin's story was that he then went home, arriving about 9:20 a.m. He was hungry, so he took some frozen hamburgers out of the freezer and cut his hand separating them with a knife. Nolin said he then went to Falmouth Hospital. After a one-and-one-half-hour wait, he left to get insurance papers from his employer.

Ever astute, Officer Smith could not help but notice the extensive scratch marks on Nolin's leg, and took a photograph of them, which was admitted into evidence. None of those present at the party recalled having seen these scratches on Friday night. Nolin's employer told Smith that the work Nolin did on Monday did not require him to crawl through any areas where he might have gotten scratched. With that, Smith asked Nolin if he could search his house looking for Wessner's cell phone. At that time, it was still just a missing person case.

He looked for Wessner's cellular telephone, but did not find it there. He also looked inside the freezer, where he saw hamburger packages. There was no indication of blood on the hamburgers or anywhere else in the house. The Falmouth police also began a search for Wessner's vehicle. It had not been seen since Saturday, when a traffic officer in Woods Hole issued two tickets for a parking violation at a meter near where the witness testified she had seen Wessner and the man in the dark pickup truck.

Smith knew that something was not right about Nolin, but he needed proof that the young, handsome golf pro had met with foul play. He got what he was looking after another Falmouth cop, Sergeant Christopher Hamilton, went fishing off the shore of Woods Hole on Wednesday, October 1, 2003. He noticed a flock of birds gathering at an area on the beach. The sight nagged at him and when he went back to work that Friday, Hamilton took another officer back to the spot where the birds had gathered. Under a pile of jagged rocks they found Wessner's remains, naked except for a single sock.

The body was decomposing and badly beaten, with severe trauma to the head and bones on both sides of the face, broken so grievously in places that the connections were completely severed. An autopsy later revealed the one-half-inch tip of a knife blade embedded in the skull. The medical examiner determined that the cause of death was sharp- and blunt-force trauma. A forensic dentist was able to identify the body as Wessner's from records. The police also searched a boathouse near where Wessner's body had been discovered. They found bloodstains matching the DNA profiles of both Wessner and Nolin at several locations in the boathouse. The next day an arrest warrant was issued in the Falmouth Division of the District Court Department and Nolin was busted.

Nolin was convicted at trial and sentenced to life in prison. It was another long and tiring case for Cape and Islands District Attorney Michael O'Keefe that played out while questions about the way he'd handled the Worthington case continued to be asked. Not only did he have to deal with the murder of a promising young golf pro, the homicide also brought the Catholic priest scandal to Cape Cod. Kelly would plead guilty to tax evasion and embezzlement charges. In his will, he left everything to Nolin, fueling the speculation that the priest and the pedophile had been lovers. There had been elaborate birthday parties thrown for Nolin by the priest at his estate. Lawyers for both men have denied they were having sex, but law enforcement officials don't buy that claim. Nonetheless, it was a sordid scandal and O'Keefe had to handle much of the detail of that murder personally because there was so much scrutiny from the press, Wessner's family and the very politically powerful archdiocese.

But the cases that puzzled O'Keefe's office stretched back as far as 2001. As the nation dealt with the aftermath of the September 11 terror attacks, Cape Cod homicide investigators were horrified by the discovery of the headless body of Kelly Ford, which was found in a shallow grave on Scusset Beach in Sandwich by two young boys playing Frisbee on October 22, 2001. Initially, investigators could not identify her remains. Her case was marked "unidentified female body found in the dunes." Then Ford's mother came forward with a photograph of a tattoo that her daughter had on her back. The inking was the Chinese symbol of "summer love." The headless body had an identical tattoo. It did not take long for her family to determine that the corpse that had been found by the boys was in fact 23-year-old Kelly Ford.

A pretty young mother of a 4-year-old, Ford had fallen into a spiral of drug addiction and alcoholism. She had pulled her life together in the summer of 2001 and had moved into a residential treatment center in hardscrabble Lynn, Massachusetts. She was on her way to a job interview in nearby Marblehead when she vanished on August 15. Her disappearance did not raise a lot of alarms. Because she was newly clean and sober, her family and friends just assumed that she was out on another tragic run with the needle and had slipped into the shadowy world of copping and using heroin in some hellhole somewhere. She probably did not even want to be found. The truth appeared to be much more sinister, however.

Alcoholics Anonymous meetings are open to everyone. And that means that some seedy characters are able to prey on young, vulnerable and shaky newcomers to the 12-step program. One such man was Eugene McCollom: convicted murderer and suspected serial killer. Months before Ford's body was found, McCollom had met a former prostitute at an AA meeting at the Chelsea Soldiers' Home, a hospital for veterans. The woman—whose real name was never discovered—was later found hacked to pieces in the woods near the hospital. McCollom admitted to having sex with her for money and was arrested for the murder months after Ford's headless body had been found. That victim's head and hands were found buried on Nahant Beach, a public beach near his room at the Greater Lynn YMCA—not far from the residential treatment center where Ford had been living. It was clear that McCollom had strangled his victim and then chopped her up in his room. The hooker's murder was tragic well beyond the painful way in which she'd died. She was so alone in her death that police released a sketch of her face in the hopes that her loved ones could identify her. No one ever did.

In the end, McCollom was convicted of the hooker's murder and confessed to killing a Lynn man whom he attended meetings with, Jackie Leyden. Leyden had been beheaded using the same "method and tools" that Ford's killer had used. McCollom led investigators to yet another beheaded body buried in a sandy beach in Florida, but to this day, he will not admit that he killed Kelly Ford.

Just weeks after Ford's headless corpse had been found, her older brother Joshua Ford was found shot dead and dismembered in a beach town in Maryland. He and his girlfriend had been partying with another couple when a heated argument turned murderous. Ford and his girlfriend were shot dead as they cowered behind a bathroom door. Their bodies were then cut into pieces and discarded at a Delaware dump.

The two homicides shattered the Ford family, lifelong residents of the tight-knit neighborhood of South Boston. After Mark Ford lost both his son and his daughter in inexplicably violent homicides, he told reporters that "he couldn't walk straight" ever again.

Cape and Islands District Attorney Michael O'Keefe will not comment on the Ford case or respond to questions about McCollom's connection to it. The Ford family, however, is certain that the serial killer who drove Kelly Ford to meetings is the man who killed her. They remind O'Keefe of that fact on a regular basis.

And just when O'Keefe, his prosecutors and his investigators thought they could come up for air, the tranquil island of Nantucket would mark its first murder in nearly a quarter century. The victim was a beautiful, vivacious millionaire businesswoman who had retreated to a quaint cottage on Nantucket—a place where she had created cherished childhood memories—to escape an abusive lover she had dated for just six weeks. That lover, Thomas Toolan III, was a charming con man who followed her from the island of Manhattan to the island of Nantucket. It was there that he bought a fishing knife from a tackle shop and broke into the cottage where the woman he briefly dated, 44-year-old Elizabeth "Beth" Lochtefeld, was staying. He stabbed her twenty-three times and left her shredded body on the floor in the front room of the cottage. His frenzied attack left some stab wounds that were four inches deep.

Toolan, a handsome blond who had at one time been a successful banker and worked as a vice president at Citigroup, met Lochtefeld in New York City on Labor Day weekend and the two became inseparable. Beth thought she might finally have found love, an elusive entity for women living in New York City after they hit 40. She gushed about her new love for weeks, telling friends, "I just love this guy." To her family she declared, "I've never been happier in my life."

Why wouldn't she love him? He was tall and solidly built with piercing blue eyes and a mesmerizing personality. He could talk about art and politics, and took Lochtefeld to the best places in Manhattan. His charisma, his charm and his preppy clothing hid the truth: that despite his tailored Brooks Brothers suits, his wealthy influential family and Ivy League degree from Columbia University, Toolan was just a liar and a booze-addled thief. In fact, Toolan had been arrested at an antiques show in 2001 at the Seventh Regiment Armory in Manhattan after New York City police said he'd tried to walk off with a 60-pound, $80,000 marble bust of a Roman aristocrat under his coat. Toolan told a security guard who stopped him that he was "just pulling a prank." That prank cost him his job at Citigroup. He sank into a pit of alcoholic despair after that. He was able to hide his desperation—until, that is, he'd had a couple of drinks. Other women who had briefly dated him remembered Toolan as the "psycho date" who appeared fine until he was intoxicated. Then he was aggressive, jealous and accusatory.

It was after a few drinks one night in October 2004 that Toolan dropped to one knee and delivered an insane, ranting marriage proposal that forced Lochtefeld to confront his inanity. She rejected his pleas to marry him, which provoked Toolan to hold her hostage in his Manhattan apartment. When he finally passed out, she fled for Nantucket and settled into a remote rented cottage. She was so rattled by Toolan's behavior, Beth went to the Nantucket police and asked about getting a protective order. She refused to be cooperative with police, and said she was just seeking information. Four days later she would be dead.

"It was clear that he creeped her out, but as far as anything else, she wasn't ready to go that far, and she wouldn't give the officer his name," Nantucket Police Chief William Pittman would later remember.

Toolan was convicted of murder in the first degree and sentenced to life in prison. He had been arrested in Rhode Island driving a rented car back toward Manhattan. He was drunk and had been arrested for driving while intoxicated when the BOLO—Be on the Lookout—for him was broadcast throughout New England. O'Keefe's office was grateful he had been captured. But there was still the slew of legal motions that vaunted defense attorney Kevin Reddington—ranked the best defense attorney in Massachusetts by *Boston* magazine in 2002—would file. All of the briefs pointed to the insanity defense Reddington planned to use in the case. He filed a "notice of lack of criminal responsibility, diminished capacity," and said that Toolan's alcohol abuse and the blackouts that came with his drinking made him not responsible for the murder.

Reddington's attempt was a good one, but it would not work. His argument that Toolan had frontal lobe brain damage caused by years of drug abuse, and complicated by depression, anxiety and dementia, failed to convince a jury comprised of year-round Nantucket residents of his client's innocence. When all else failed, Reddington pulled out the oldest trick in the defense attorneys' magic hat: blame the victim. Beth Lochtefeld had ultimately been responsible for her own murder because she'd pushed her lover over the edge when she rebuked his proposal.

Reddington was good, and O'Keefe knew it, expending a lot of resources going up against him in the Toolan case even if it did appear to be an open-and-shut case of a despondent whacko going off the deep end after he'd been dumped. So when Shirley Reine was murdered in 2005, O'Keefe was already a very busy man.

John Busby certainly did not care about Michael O'Keefe's heavy caseload. For him it was maddening that the district attorney who should want to see someone who'd blasted a cop in the face with buckshot doing time seemed more concerned about the reports that could make the Falmouth Police Department look bad. Busby was furious that O'Keefe would deny him access to the reports filed after the sons of the Falmouth Fox, Todd and Melvin Jr., had confessed their roles in his shooting to police. Busby became apoplectic when John Reine confessed to being the driver that night. Certainly the former cop understood that it had become an embarrassment that Falmouth allowed Melvin Reine to run amok. Worse were the allegations that some of the town's police officers had tarnished their badges protecting him. Busby felt like O'Keefe only made the situation worse with his steadfast refusal to let anyone look at the reports. *What was he trying to hide?*

O'Keefe's actions lent credence to the feelings some officers had that if reports became public, the information contained in them would shine a very bright spotlight on the dirty little secret of police corruption that had been allowed to fester in Falmouth for decades. Certainly, questions would be raised about why Busby's shooting had not been solved and why criminal cases involving Melvin Reine would vanish just like his first wife and his 17-year-old employee Paul Alwardt had.

After Shirley Reine was murdered in 2005, her sister, Loretta Gilfoy, would hit on that very point, saying: "Falmouth is not the sweet little town everyone thinks it is."

She was just as angry as John Busby was about Melvin's one-man crime wave.

"Maybe if they had done something about Melvin years ago, my sister would be alive right now. Or she might have been able to die in her sleep. Anything is better than what happened to her. Everyone knew what Melvin was up to. They should have done something about it."

Falmouth police brass had missed the perfect opportunity "to do something about Melvin" in the days after John Busby was nearly shot dead. Melvin Reine had crossed a line when he blew off Busby's face—a crime for which the Falmouth Fox was never charged. A crime for which John Busby will never, ever see justice.

The Reine compound, marked by a stone with the family name etched under a trash truck, is the scene of many crimes. Shirley Reine was shot dead in the home she shared with Melvin Reine; John Busby, the Falmouth cop who was shot in the face, arrested one of Melvin's many children in the driveway. John Reine, who would give up his brother in connection with Busby's shooting, still lives here.

Photo by Michele McPhee

Fox weathervane that Melvin Reine used to taunt local police. He fully embraced his nickname "The Falmouth Fox."

Photo by Michele McPhee

Wanda Medeiros Reine with her boys, Melvin Jr. (left) and Todd (on lap).
From the Reine family photo album, provided by Todd Reine

Shirley Reine as a young woman.
Provided by Loretta Gilfoy

Shirley Reine after her arrest in 2002.

The main house on the Reine compound and the garage where Shirley Reine was murdered on May 10, 2005.

Photo by Michele McPhee

Mug shot of Melvin Reine in 2007.

A view of the cranberry bog in front of the Reine compound where Jeff Flanagan's body was found.

Photo by Michele McPhee

Rick Smith in 1982 on duty in Falmouth.
Provided by Rick Smith

Busby compound after the shooting (the fence was built for the family's protection).
Provided by Rick Smith

Rick Smith and his wife Terry along with John and Polly Busby in Falmouth in summer of 2008.

Provided by Rick Smith

John Reine, Melvin's brother, who admitted to being the getaway driver in the shooting of John Busby.

Melvine Reine Jr. who, along with his brother Todd, was suing Shirley Reine over his father's business.

Mug shot of Todd Reine taken after his arrest in connection with the home invasion that took place at his stepmother's home. He was convicted of setting up the robbery to obtain his father's will.

Mug shot of John Rams, who told police Todd Reine wanted Shirley Reine dead. Rams broke into Shirley's home.

Mug shot of Nadia Simuliac, John Rams' girlfriend. She later became romantically linked to Todd Reine. Her conviction as the getaway driver for the robbery of Shirley Reine's home is on appeal.

TWELVE

John Busby might not ever see anyone locked up for blowing off his face, but at the very least he could expose the complete lack of action taken on his behalf by the Falmouth Police Department, the Cape and Islands District Attorney's Office and lawmakers on Boston's Beacon Hill. Busby's move would provoke a disgraceful display of petty politics and exemplify the classic blame-shifting that Massachusetts politicians were famous for. There are hundreds and hundreds of bills filed on Boston's Beacon Hill promising to protect the citizens of the Commonwealth of Massachusetts every single year. Only a fraction of those bills ever saw their way to being signed. One that would languish in the State House was John Busby's attempt to extend the statute of limitations for crimes committed against police officers from seven years to twenty. It was a reasonable request that would arm police and prosecutors with the tools they needed to go after anyone who tried to kill a cop. A year after Busby had been shot, a grand jury was convened to hear evidence in the case, and Melvin Reine was called in to testify, along with his friend, Falmouth cop Michael Leighton, who'd failed a lie detector test about the Busby shooting and the involvement of the Falmouth Fox. But the case never went anywhere. The investigation was a sham and a disgrace, and Busby wanted to make sure nothing like that would ever happen to another cop.

On November 1, 2005, Busby walked up the marble stairs

into the Massachusetts State House. The The building is topped with a golden dome that glows under the sunlight and can be seen for miles. Busby now covered his wound with a scraggly beard, still red in some places as a reminder of his youth, and gray in others, which belied the long years he and his family had spent on the run, hiding from the Falmouth Fox. He was flanked by one of the crusaders, his good friend Rick Smith. Busby could not shake that feeling of rage, the fury that fueled him to live long enough to see Melvin Reine locked up, an anger that had since dissipated and had been channeled into trying to change the law that had let him down. Busby certainly had the support of Falmouth cops who serve on the job today. (In 2005, one of the men suspected of helping the Falmouth Fox, Arturo Monteiro, had passed away. Leighton was off the job and continued to deny any involvement. Ferreira was gone and refused to talk about his old job as the Falmouth Police Chief. Mustafa was a town selectman.)

Busby also had the support of a former Falmouth town official who had become a state representative, Eric Turkington, who filed the bill on Busby's behalf. Busby thanked Turkington as he took the floor before the Joint Committee on Judiciary that November morning. The state representative sat to Busby's left at a long, wooden table; Cape and Islands District Attorney Michael O'Keefe sat on his right.

Settled into his hard, wooden chair, he moved his mouth closer to the microphone. Then he began speaking, each word pronounced as if Busby had had to chew through glass before it would leave his mouth.

"For me, an extension of the statute of limitations for assaults against police officers going from ten years to thirty years comes too late to bring justice to those who attempted to murder me in 1979. Evidence has recently come forward in the way of confessions identifying my assailants; this new evidence comes twenty-six years after the assault against me. However, the current ten-year statute of limitations prevents any legal action to my perpetrators. I do not want other police officers who are the victims of violent crimes prevented from seeking justice distributed to anyone committing an assault against them," Busby said.

The short statement took him about eight minutes. He struggled over every word. Legislators strained to hear him.

"This law would send a strong message to the public that an assault against a police officer will carry with it a greater chance of being prosecuted," Busby said. "The injuries I sustained from the assault against me with a gunshot wound through and through my jaw makes it difficult for me to be as articulate as I would like."

Busby paused. It was difficult for him to contemplate that he was a weaker version of himself. Long gone was the rough-and-tumble Falmouth police officer who could run miles along the Cape Cod shoreline. Gone were the sinewy muscles and the lead-lined leather gloves and the "Prosecutor" nightstick he carried to keep thugs in line. He could barely talk, and the people he was trying to reach with his statement could barely hear him.

"I apologize if I am difficult to understand. I will live the rest of my life with a portion of my face, jaw, teeth, and tongue missing. Those injuries, along with the increased chance of choking when I eat, and the lack of control of my saliva, remind me all day, every day, of the assault against me.

"Please do the right thing and make this bill a law."

Outside the courthouse, Busby massaged his tired face. Some days it felt like the explosions that ripped apart his jaw had happened just a few days earlier. He then mused to reporters who gathered around him like a flock of pigeons about to pounce on a crumb:

"The worst thing is, my family loves Cape Cod. We loved it," Busby said. "And now we can never go back there. We can never feel safe."

The bill has since languished with no action. It was a simple filing, and one that would be submitted by Turkington every year after Busby's testimony in 2005:

HOUSE . . . . **No. 1748**

By Mr. Turkington of Falmouth, petition of Eric Turkington and others for legislation to extend the statute of limitations for certain crimes committed against police officers. The Judiciary.

The Commonwealth of Massachusetts

PETITION OF:

Eric Turkington   Matthew C. Patrick
Robert A. O'Leary   Cleon H. Turner
Therese Murray

In the Year Two Thousand and Seven.

AN ACT EXTENDING THE STATUTE OF LIMITATIONS FOR CERTAIN CRIMES COMMITTED AGAINST POLICE OFFICERS.

Be it enacted by the Senate and House of Representatives in General Court assembled, and by the authority of the same, as follows:

1 Section 63 of chapter 277 of the General Laws, as ap-
   pearing in
2 the 2002 Official Edition, is hereby amended by adding at the end
3 thereof the following sentence:—
4 "Notwithstanding the foregoing provisions, if a victim
   of a crime,
5 for an offense set forth in section thirteen A, thirteen
   D, fifteen, and
6 fifteen A of chapter 265 of the General Laws, or conspiracy to
7 commit any of said offense or as an accessory thereto,
   is a police

8 officer, an indictment may be found and filed within
   thirty years of
9 commission of such offense."

But House Bill No. 1748 would never go anywhere. Apparently, none of the lawmakers in attendance at Busby's testimony remembered how painful it was for him to get out his words through his mangled, maimed jaw that November day. Aside from the three legislators and Senate President Therese Murray, not a single lawmaker would sign on to the bill. Lawmakers did not do the right thing by John Busby; and by refusing to release the confessions of Melvin Jr., Todd and John Reine—even to the wounded cop—the district attorney did not do the right thing either. That was the Massachusetts norm when it came to passing legislation that would benefit crime victims rather than perpetrators. A large majority of the state representatives on Beacon Hill were defense attorneys, and they made it difficult for common-sense laws—like Jessica's Law, which was passed in roughly two dozen states and would give judges mandatory minimums in child sex abuse cases, and Melanie's Law, which targeted repeat drunk drivers—to pass. It was infuriating to a lot of police officers and prosecutors, but Massachusetts voters notoriously elected the same liberals into office year after year. And those liberal elected officials would in turn appoint liberal judges to oversee criminal cases. As a result, the state of Massachusetts had become a national laughing-stock. New Hampshire newspapers wrote editorials calling the state "Laxachusetts."

The *New Hampshire Union Leader* complained: "When thugs commit crimes in Massachusetts, too often it is New Hampshire that gets punished." The paper explained that "Massachusetts enters only about 5 percent of its outstanding warrants into the [FBI's National Crime Information Center] database." Consequently, 95 percent of criminals wanted in Massachusetts appear law-abiding when New Hampshire cops stop them and compare their names against this database. Governor Mitt Romney proposed a bill to require state and local cops to report such warrants to the FBI, but failed to get it through his state legislature.

"People tragically have been killed over this," Stephen Monier, New Hampshire's U.S. Marshal told the *Union Leader*. "It's a huge issue."

It was well-known across the country that scumbags, pedophiles, rapists and killers often got a pass if they were sentenced in Massachusetts. That's if they were even caught. It was not just the arsonists like Melvin Reine who got out early. The release of a man who'd hacked his own mother to death would derail the presidential aspirations of former Massachusetts Republican Governor Mitt Romney.

Daniel Tavares was a butcher with a long rap sheet when he stabbed his mother to death in 1991. Behind bars, he was housed in the Disciplinary Disorders Unit at Walpole. If Walpole housed the state's most violent, the "DDU" was home to the worst of the worst inmates in the state. Behind bars, Tavares was charged with attacking correction officers and other prisoners. Before he killed his mother, he had been busted eight different times on robbery and drug charges, including an arrest for a violent home invasion and the stabbing of a neighbor. But for some inexplicable reason, Tavares was released from prison despite the objections of prosecutors. At a "dangerousness hearing" they tried to keep him behind bars, saying that he continued to be a danger to society and had an open criminal case against him for assaulting two correction officers in separate incidents. In one case, Tavares punched a guard in the head and yelled, "I'm going to kill you!" In another, he spat in the eye of a guard who had tried to slip him a meal plate. During his time in prison, he was also quite prolific. He wrote up a hit list of people he wanted to assassinate, including his own father, Attorney General Tom Reilly and Mitt Romney. After he announced his candidacy, Mitt Romney's security staff of Massachusetts State Troopers and Secret Service agents were apprised of the threats—but no one else was.

Romney's hand-picked judicial appointee Kathe Tuttman

ruled that she could see "no proof" that Tavares was dangerous, and overturned a lower court's bail. Tavares was released on personal recognizance. Tuttman also spurned
prosecutors' wishes that Tavares wear a monitoring brace-
let. "There is no indication," she ruled, "that he is a risk of
flight." Tuttman ordered Tavares to report to a probation officer thrice weekly, work as a welder at a Massachusetts
company called Davon Steel and move in with his sister in
Dighton, Massachusetts. None of that would happen. His
sister said she'd had no idea that Daniel Tavares was supposed to move in. Instead, Tavares took off, went west and
married Jennifer Lynn Freitas, 37, a Washington woman he
met on a convict version of Match.com—inmateconnections.
com. The two had corresponded while Tavares had been incarcerated and exchanged nuptials after his release, moving
into a trailer near Graham, Washington, some 45 miles south
of Seattle. Freitas was apparently smitten with the killer's
web ad, in which he described himself as an "albino alliga-
tor" looking for love.

Months later Tavares got into a dispute with his two neighbors, Beverly Mauck, 28, and Brian Mauck, 30, a young
couple who liked scuba diving and had married in the Turks
and Caicos just a year earlier. Tavares was enraged that Brian
Mauck did not want to pay him $500 for a tattoo sketch he
had drawn. Police say Tavares wrapped a .22-caliber revolver in a towel, kicked in the Maucks' door and then fa-
tally shot each of them three times in the head. Detectives
say they matched Tavares to a bloody palm print and shoe
prints found in the Maucks' home. Tavares has since confessed to the murders and is awaiting trial.

Romney entered into the fray by attacking his own judicial appointment, saying that Judge Tuttman's decision
"showed an inexplicable lack of good judgment in a hearing
that decided to put someone on the street who had not only
in the past been convicted of manslaughter, but had threatened the lives of other individuals and was a flight risk. And
I think on that basis, that despite her record as being a law-

and-order prosecutor, her lack of judgment suggests that she needs to resign from that post."

When Romney had appointed Tuttman, however, he seemed more focused on gender issues than on law and order. Tuttman was one of four associate justices nominated in April 2006—all women. All four had prosecutorial experience. In fact, Tuttman, a registered Democrat, was an Essex County assistant district attorney who, among others, prosecuted Eugene McCollom, the serial killer who continues to be the prime suspect in the murder of Kelly Ford, the recovering drug addict whose headless body was found buried in the dunes of Scusset Beach in Sandwich.

Romney dropped out of the race, as stories about Massachusetts convicts causing murder and mayhem in other states continued to plague him.

"It's because of stupidity in Massachusetts that my daughter is dead," Beverly Mauck's father, Darrel Slater said in the days after his daughter was slain. "How does a guy who killed his mother, get charged with more crimes, get out of jail? How can he leave the state?"

It was a question that would be asked over and over again. Another Massachusetts ex-con released during the Romney administration, 26-year-old Michael "Stix" Addison, is now facing the death penalty for assassinating a Manchester, NH, police officer with a single bullet to the head. The family of the slain cop, Officer Michael Briggs, was stunned to learn that Addison had a lengthy criminal history that included a charge that he'd tried to kill someone when he was 16 years old. In that attack, he'd pointed a gun at a classmate and pulled the trigger—twice. The gun misfired. Then, a day after his 17th birthday in 1997, Addison knifed a basketball player in Roxbury. He was charged with assault and battery with intent to murder and armed assault, and tried as a result. A Massachusetts judge sentenced him to a whopping 3 years, freeing Addison again in 2000. He violated his probation four months later, according to court records, but was never put back in prison. Briggs, one of Manchester's Finest, paid the ultimate price after the state of Massachusetts paid little or no attention to Addison's well-documented penchant for violence and bloodletting.

Before Romney could drop out of the race, a nutcase stormed Democrat candidate and New York Senator Hillary Clinton's campaign headquarters in New Hampshire with what looked like a dynamite bomb strapped to his waist. After taking five terrified campaign volunteers hostage, Leeland Eisenberg said he would release them only if he got an audience with Senator Clinton. A New Hampshire SWAT team smoked him out five hours after his caper began and none of his captives was injured. No one in New Hampshire was surprised to learn that Eisenberg was a twice-convicted rapist from Massachusetts and a man who had sued the Boston Archdiocese claiming that he had been raped by a pedophile priest. Worse, Eisenberg had raped one woman while he was a fugitive. He was serving time for an unconnected rape he'd committed in the 1980s when he slipped out of a Massachusetts treatment center for criminal sexual deviants and raped again. It would be unbelievable if it was not Massachusetts.

None of this was far from John Busby's mind as he prepared his testimony. He knew how despicable criminals were shown more rights in Massachusetts than their victims. He knew that liberal, ACLU types fought for the convicts in Massachusetts more than for the civilians. Busby had seen firsthand how leniently some suspects would be handled; how some career criminals were allowed to expand their control of small towns the way Reine had with Falmouth. But Busby was not the type of man who gave up easily. He was determined that the horror show that had been inflicted on his family would not happen to another cop. Massachusetts lawmakers would have to sleep with rocks in their pillows if they did not pass legislation that would deter violent attacks on police officers. Apparently, most of the legislators were okay with that. Busby was determined to try.

Reports as juicy as the ones detailing confessions and police corruption are often leaked. There are the malcontents tired of the powers that be and those who remained hell-bent on making the guilty pay. That would be the case with the Reine reports (which were given to this writer by a law enforcement source).

Maybe someone with access to the reports was pushed too far by remarks made by Todd Reine days after Busby testified at the State House.

"Busby needs to stop crying," Todd Reine said. "He took on the local gunslinger and he lost."

In short order, however, Todd Reine would be the one crying. His beloved uncle, a man who'd helped raise him during the years his father was incarcerated for his arson spree in Falmouth decades earlier, would soon spill his guts. An angry and embarrassed district attorney who needed to appease *Cape Cod Times* reporters who wrote relentless investigative pieces about the Falmouth Fox and his children would make sure that at least one Reine would land in prison. That would eventually become Todd Reine. He would be arrested for orchestrating a crime against his stepmother: the burglary of her home. Investigators hoped Todd Reine would eventually be charged with the crime they believed he'd committed, or was responsible for: Shirley Reine's murder.

THIRTEEN

Detective Kent Clarkson looked up from his desk at the Falmouth Police Department for the men he had been expecting all afternoon. It was June 14, 2002, at 4:14 p.m. when Reine brothers Melvin Jr. and Todd walked into the detective division to talk about the Busby shooting. Clarkson had his materials ready. A tape recorder had been set on a table in front of him. A box of materials relating to the unsolved cold case the Reine boys claimed to have information on was next to his feet. It was not as heavy as it should have been. That's because there had not been a lot of reports written in 1979. No detailed interviews with potential suspects conducted in the days after Busby's face was reconstructed by surgeons. There were the cursory police reports, of course. But nothing about Ferreira's resignation, or the fact that Busby's family had had to hire an attack dog. Nothing about the cops, the crusaders, who'd had to accompany Busby's kids to school. Nothing about the fact that every noise, every odd look from a stranger would give Polly anxiety. Nothing about the nonstop moving to states where the Busbys did not have friends or family. Nothing about the knowledge Busby had been forced to live with for the rest of his days: it was very likely that fellow cops had helped the man who wanted him dead.

The newest incident report to be entered into evidence in the case was given a numbered code: I0301168. The victim's name—John Busby—was scrawled on the side of a box containing relevant materials. But there was yet another victim listed on the report that Detective Clarkson was about to fill in with details provided by the Reine brothers. Her name was Polly Busby, John's wife.

It was an appropriate description to call her a victim even though she had not been shot. She had married a young, vibrant, handsome man whose face would be wrecked by buckshot and who, for a very long time, had to be fed by injecting food into his stomach lining. A man who at age 34 would lose his muscle mass because of the fact that he would never be able to eat a solid meal again. A man who could no longer burst into song without notice or scream at his kids to stop horsing around. A man who became so consumed by hatred and revenge that his wife had to worry about not only his health, but his sanity.

Polly, at the time of Detective Clarkson's report, was only 58. But there were days when she felt a lot older than that. Who wouldn't feel tired and weary after they'd uprooted their entire family and settled into a rural Southern town without any support of friends? Who wouldn't feel old after they'd spent decades wondering if the people who'd wanted her husband dead would come back for her and her three kids? All she wanted was a little bit of justice for John, and she was hoping that someone might have been able to give her at least that.

As the Reine boys began to talk, Clarkson flipped on the tape recorder. In the room was State Trooper John Kotfila from the Cape and Islands District Attorney's Office. O'Keefe had sent him. Even though the Reine brothers had come in before their stepmother had been shot dead—in fact, many would believe that their entire motivation in sitting down with investigators stemmed from their hatred for Shirley—they were the sons of the Falmouth Fox. Who knew what kind of information could be gleaned from that interview?

Even in a professional setting, police could not help but think of the adult Reine children as "the boys." That was how Clarkson would later type it in on that numbered incident report. It would also help investigators obtain a search warrant for Shirley Reine's home. It was not as if she was necessarily a target, and by then her husband had been locked up in the mental ward of Taunton State Hospital. Still, there was no telling what kind of evidence could be stumbled upon. Something that might have appeared innocuous could have real value to the investigators who were still saddled with the unsolved murder of Shirley's ex-boyfriend Charles Flanagan; or the disappearance of Melvin Reine's first wife, Wanda; or the vanished employee who'd never disembarked from the Martha's Vineyard ferry. Those case files were not tossed or forgotten. They were part of a high pile of cold cases that still demanded attention from an overburdened detective squad.

So Clarkson may not have been ready to believe every word that Melvin Reine Jr. and his younger brother Todd had to say that afternoon, but he was more than ready to hear them out. As the boys talked, Clarkson listened. Then he listened again as he typed up his report.

On June 14, 2002 I met with Melvin Reine Jr. and Todd Reine in reference to criminal activity that their father Melvin Reine Sr. and his wife Reine had been involved in over the past several years dating back to the 1970s. The boys were time and date specific on several events that were supported with evidence pursuant to search warrants executed on diverse dates throughout 2002.

Melvin Reine Jr. began to explain facts pertaining to the shooting of Falmouth Police Officer John Busby on August 31, 1979 on Sandwich Road in Falmouth. Melvin Reine Jr. stated that he was at his home at 657 East Falmouth Highway weeks prior to the shooting when he heard his father Melvin Reine Jr. and his uncle John Reine planning the attack on Officer John Busby on several different occasions. Melvin Reine Jr. stated that John Reine had several confrontations with Officer Busby and on one occasion John Reine attempted to drive Officer Busby over at fatality (David Riley) in front of what was the Big Fisherman at the time on East Falmouth Highway. Officer Busby charged

John Reine with assault but could not leave his post at the fatality to pursue and arrested him on that evening.

Melvin Reine Jr. explained to Trooper Kotfila and I that the motivation of the shooting was to see that Officer Busby would not be able to testify in the upcoming trial of John Reine. John Reine was driving a tractor trailer at the time for Stop and Shop and if he was convicted of the charge, he would lose his license and hence his job. Melvin Reine Jr. stated that his father Melvin Reine Sr. received the schedule of Officer Busby from Officer Arthur Monteiro [since deceased] of the Falmouth Police Department. Officer Monteiro helped Reine Sr. because he was unhappy with Busby's physical handling of one of his family members in recent weeks.

Melvin Reine Jr. explained to both investigators that on the evening of August 31, 1979 Melvin Sr. left his residence at 657 East Falmouth Highway with his brother John Reine in a dark blue Ford station wagon with wood paneling on the sides. Melvin Jr. stated that the station wagon belonged to his father Melvin Sr. Melvin Jr. stated that his father gave him specific instructions on the night of the 31st to stay and monitor the police scanner, more specifically the Falmouth Police frequency. Reine Sr. explained to Melvin Jr. that he wanted him to listen to every transmission and write everything the cruisers and the station said down on some paper for him to look at when he returned. Melvin Reine Jr. stated that when his Uncle John and his father returned to the house, they asked Melvin Jr. about everything that was said on the scanner. Melvin Jr. explained that his Uncle John and his father were explaining to him when they returned how they let the Busby vehicle pass at first because there was a vehicle in the area that was similar to his and the Busby vehicle had fresh paint on it. Melvin Sr. stated that they pulled in behind the Busby vehicle. The fact that the Busby vehicle had different paint on it threw them off and they weren't able to shoot him in the area of Sandwich Road that they had planned on that their time table was thrown off a little bit because of the uncertainty. Melvin Jr. stated that his Uncle John Reine was driving his father's station wagon and his father was lying in the rear of the station wagon with the shotgun and shot Officer Busby. Shirley Souza was in the front passenger's seat.

Melvin Reine Jr. explained that his Uncle John Reine had gone to a friend's house in the New Bedford area named "Navajo Joe" and borrowed a pump and borrowed a pump shotgun from him. Melvin Jr. stated that his uncle brought the shotgun back to Navajo Joe (Henry Silva) after the assault on Officer Busby. Both Todd Reine and Melvin Reine stated that "Navajo Joe" was a truck driver and drove on the West Coast for approximately ten years off and on. When Navajo Joe and John Reine both drove for Stop and Shop is when they became friends and made the connection for the shotgun.

On December 5, 2002 Detective Robidoux and I traveled to Fall River, MA in an attempt to locate Henry Silva AKA Navajo Joe at the last known address the registry of motor vehicles had for him. We arrived at 322 South Beacon Street in an effort to locate Silva. We spoke to several neighbors and found that Mrs. Silva came home for lunch frequently so we parked across the street and waited. Approximately ½ hour later a vehicle pulled into the Silva Yard. We approached the female who identified herself as Mrs. Silva. We made an inquiry about her husband Henry Silva and she stated that he was flying in from Arizona and would be in late and she would advise him that we would be back in the morning to speak to him.

On December 6, 2002 we arrived at the Silva dwelling at approximately 11:30 with two detectives from the Fall River Police Department. We asked Mr. Silva to come and speak with us at the Fall River Department about a case that we were investigating that we felt he may have some information on. Mr. Silva agreed to speak with us and followed us to the police department in his own vehicle. We entered a briefing room with Mr. Silva and explained why we wished to speak with him. We explained that we were looking into Melvin Reine and asked him what his relationship with the Reine family was.

Mr. Silva began by explaining that he was friendly with John Reine because of their mutual employer Stop & Shop from 1972 to 1979. He left in either late '79 or early '80. He couldn't recall exactly. He stated that he and John were friendly and would get together frequently socially. He stated that he told Johnny that his wife was being unfaithful to him and they had a falling out after that and were not very friendly. He stated that John used to call him every Christmas but he hasn't spoken to him in approximately 7–8 years. He stated that he spoke to him briefly on the CB a few weeks ago but John was quick and not very friendly to him. He stated that he had not been to John Reine's house in 15–16 years.

I asked him about his relationship with Melvin Reine Sr. and he stated the he didn't really get along with Melvin. Silva stated that Melvin lived next door and he would see him when he was at Johnnies but he didn't care for him. He stated that Johnnie was sociable and joking around and Melvin was always acting nutty. Stated that he used to see Melvin's two boys in the yard working on their cars but never really had much contact with them.

I explained to Silva that our department in conjunction with the state police were looking into the shooting of a police officer in 1979 and his name had come up in the investigation and we wanted to ask him specific questions about his possible involvement. It was obvious that Silva was confused and had no inclination of what we were talking about.

I asked Silva if he knew anything about a shotgun that was reported to have belonged to him. He immediately responded that he had given a shotgun to John Reine. When asked for a time frame on when, he thought for a few minutes and stated that he believed it was in 1979. He stated, "Uh, ya it was in 1979, late summer I think. He came up and met me in the truck at my house in Freetown and I gave him the shotgun." Silva stated that John asked him if he had a shotgun and when he responded that he did, John asked him if he could use it because he was going hunting with his brother Melvin. Silva stated that he no longer has the weapon, but he had sold it in the early eighties to a former band member that he did not remember. He could not recall whether it was a 12-gauge shotgun or a 20-gauge but he stated that he would attempt to locate the info and get it to us.

Silva stated that he was living in Freeport at the time off exit 9, Parker Drive Area. He stated that John Reine had the weapon approximately 3 to 4 weeks prior to returning it. He stated that when John Reine gave him the weapon back he didn't check it and he didn't recall if Reine said anything when he returned it. Silva stated that he traded the gun for a microphone with the unidentified father of one of the band members that played drums (Jerry).

Silva went on to speak about coming down the Cape and all the times that he had with Johnnie Reine. Stated that he had gone to Johnnie's other brother's home several times. They called that brother "Billy Goat." Billy Goat is Manuel Reine.

The information was startling. The details on the gun used were correct. But of course, any ballistic evidence obtained after Busby's shooting was lost. It was not in the box of evidence that investigators at the Falmouth Police Department were privy to. Melvin Jr.'s recall of the information dispatched over the police scanner was uncanny. The fact that their uncle was the wheelman in the case surprised the cops. John Reine did not have a reputation like his brother. He was known as a hardworking family man who largely kept to himself. It would take police—and the Reine boys—nine months to convince John Reine that he had better cooperate with detectives as well. After all, now he had been implicated in a murder conspiracy by his nephews. A longtime friend had perfect recall about the time frame in which John Reine borrowed a shotgun from him, the late summer of 1979. John Busby had been shot on August 31, 1979. Besides, the statute of limitations on Busby's shooting had expired more than a decade earlier, so under the letter of Massachusetts law, John Reine could not be charged with murder conspiracy—even though it seemed pretty clear that he had been involved in one. John Reine had nothing to lose. Besides, he could extract revenge on his brother Melvin.

Melvin had become so twisted, and so concerned that John Reine would fold and tell the police everything about the Busby shooting, that he went as far as to send a threatening message to his brother weeks after the ambush of the Falmouth cop. As a result of Melvin's implied—and eventually very real—threats, John Reine had become as afraid of Melvin Reine as anyone else in town. The siblings had been embroiled in a land dispute after Melvin Reine built a sprawling garage on the compound, on property that belonged to John, without anyone's permission. When John Reine complained, Melvin gave him a look and snarled:

"Who's going to stop me? Not you, John, huh? You're on the road a lot of the time."

John Reine knew exactly what that threat implied. He could not be there to protect his wife if Melvin "smelled smoke," or "dropped a dime," or any of the other acts of violence the Falmouth Fox had followed through with after delivering those taunts. He would not put it past his brother to set a blaze at his home, even if it was adjacent to the Falmouth Fox's own house on the family compound. He was that crazy.

"Melvin would burn my house down with my wife in it and not even care about it," John Reine told his nephews at one point. In fact, John told police that Melvin Reine had told him in the past that he set fires, not to get sexual gratification, but to "give the cops something to do."

Besides, the two brothers had not talked much after the Busby shooting. None of Melvin Reine's siblings had much to do with him, in fact. John Reine steered clear of his brother after Melvin snarled at him and warned him to keep his mouth shut because they were "looking at jail, looking at jail." Melvin, John Reine believed, took his threat a step further.

Just weeks after the Busby shooting, John Reine was driving through Attleboro, Massachusetts, in his own personal car when he tried to swerve out of the way of an oncoming car. He almost did not succeed. A mechanic would tell him he was lucky to be alive. The steering bolt in his car had been removed. Sure, John Reine had been in a major accident, but he survived. He could not help but notice that his brother Melvin was surprised to see him when he got home that night.

"Melvin wanted me out of the way," John Reine would say of the accident. "He sabotaged my truck. I watched Melvin after that."

John Reine told friends and family members that he'd talked to police because of his deteriorating relationship with his brother Melvin. He felt he had to defend himself, not just from the judgment of people close to him—he was worried about what his fellow Cape Verdeans would think. Cape Verdeans are nothing if they are not insular. The people who immigrated to Massachusetts from Cape Verde were a hardworking bunch who lived for church, community and family. When something went wrong in the Cape Verdean community, it was usually handled from within. The police were rarely called in to resolve disputes. John Reine had been brought up to believe that was the appropriate way to handle his affairs, even with family members. This time, though, Melvin had gone too far. He'd dragged him into a murder conspiracy against a police officer. John Reine was not going to go down alone for Busby's shooting while his brother napped in a hospital ward for the criminally insane.

John Reine also told other people close to him that he was moved by his nephews' push to find out new information about their missing mother, to spark a renewed interest in her disappearance. The boys told him over and over all they wanted was to give their mother a "proper resting place." Because her remains had never been recovered, even if she had long been considered dead, Wanda Medeiros was not buried after a Catholic funeral Mass, which she would have wanted. There was no gravesite to visit. No way to pay respects.

"Give her a proper resting place, Uncle John," is how Todd Reine explained it to him. "You liked my mother. She deserves that."

John Reine had liked Wanda. And he made no secret of the fact that he'd never, ever been fond of Shirley. Not when she was a promiscuous teenager. Not when she'd first married Melvin. Not even the night of the Busby shooting as she sat in the front seat without saying a word. He remembered Shirley cleaning the Cadillac the day Jeff Flanagan's body had been fished out of the cranberry bog and how Shirley would chat up Paul Alwardt when the teen moved into the Reine compound.

"Shirley is an evil person. She's evil, boy," John Reine said.

In the end it was sweet Wanda's face that prompted him to sit down with investigators on March 31, 2003. That was a woman who never harmed a soul, who loved her sons and had been good to Melvin from the time she was just a teen-aged girl with very little experience in love affairs. John Reine remembered all too well how Melvin was when he returned home from Walpole and became mesmerized by the teenager who lived across the street. He watched as Shirley Souza's visits began as sporadic and then swelled until she was the full-time babysitter, a babysitter no one who lived on the Reine compound thought Wanda even needed, considering how devoted she was to those boys. He was pretty sure that the leggy babysitter was no innocent, and he knew that his brother Melvin had come home from prison a changed man. He did not want to believe there was anything untoward going on between the pretty teen and his older brother, but when Wanda vanished, John Reine's nagging suspicions appeared to have been corroborated.

From the day Wanda's mother showed up at the Reine compound hysterical and screeching at Melvin, "Where is my daughter?" John was convinced that the Falmouth Fox had made sure that his wife met some sort of foul play so it would be easier for him to move in the babysitter. As the years passed, John Reine also became convinced that Shirley Reine probably had something to do with Wanda's disappearance as well. He would often be overheard bemoaning— sometimes to family members, or his wife, or even to himself under his breath—caustic remarks about Shirley. His favorite line was "Shirley is an evil girl."

Despite the obvious evil that was inflicted upon Wanda Medeiros-Reine, her brother Roman still enjoyed a friendly relationship with her sons, his nephews. Of course that meant that Roman "Skip" Medeiros would be seen as a bit odd by his fellow cops on the Falmouth police force.

"It was a bit strange," State Trooper Kris Bohnenberger would later remember. "As far as we were concerned, something terrible had happened to Skip's sister, and you would see Skip chatting with Melvin like they were longtime buddies. It was definitely strange that Skip could even look at a guy who very likely had something to do with his sister disappearing."

The trooper—who would, he would claim, himself become a target of Melvin Reine's after the Falmouth Fox tried to hire a local junkie to kill him—said he could recall a day that he'd driven past one of the Five Star Enterprise trash trucks and was surprised at the scene. There was Melvin Reine behind the wheel. Standing on the truck's panel next to the driver's seat was Skip Medeiros, in uniform, sharing a laugh with his former brother-in-law. The sight of it startled Bohnenberger. "I don't think I could be laughing with the guy who was probably responsible for making my sister disappear," he would remark to other cops like his friend Rick Smith.

Bohnenberger's father had also been on the Mashpee police force and later on the State Police and had been one of the crusaders against the Falmouth Fox. Kris remembered his dad talking about the search parties that had been launched after Wanda went missing in 1971. Some of those missions looking for her were led by her brother Roman, who looked heartbroken as he made his way through the wooded areas around the Reine compound and peered into the waters around the property. When police ripped up that newly poured concrete, it was Roman Medeiros who stood in the background with his arms folded over his chest. When they searched the Reine-owned dump looking for her remains after a fire had been set there, Medeiros was in the backdrop monitoring every move of the cadaver dogs and investigators from the state police and the Falmouth detective squad. There were even quiet searches, searches that may not have been sanctioned by a judge, at some of the surrounding towns' dumps and at sites where Melvin Reine had worked as a contractor. But Wanda Medeiros Reine would never have a funeral Mass. Her body would never be found. Certainly, there was a lot of bad blood between Medeiros' mother and Melvin Reine. She never recovered from the loss of her daughter. She seemed to age a year for every day that Wanda was gone. Medeiros was certainly resentful that not only did he lose his sister, but his mother was slipping away from the family as well, her spirit dampened by grief and that awful gnawing panic of not knowing exactly what had happened.

As the years passed, it seemed the men buried the hatchet, perhaps for the sake of Todd and Melvin Jr. After all, Medeiros knew that they needed a solid man in their lives. Shirley was just a teenager and she was raising the boys. Melly was only 7 when his mother did not come home; Todd was 6. Melvin was working all the time. Their Uncle John was close, but he was on the road a lot. They needed the influence of a man like Roman "Skip" Medeiros, and he felt obligated to be there for his sister's kids. So he was.

Then, in 1983 it seemed that the relationship between the Falmouth Fox and the Falmouth police captain had deteriorated once again. Retired police officers still can remember that night. There was a call dispatched that Melvin Reine had rear-ended a cruiser that had been driven by Medeiros. The accident was completely unprovoked. It appeared that

Reine saw Medeiros driving the cruiser, pressed the gas pedal and rammed the cruiser from behind. Medeiros, for some reason, did not give chase. He did not broadcast the attack over the police radio or call for help. Later that night, a cop was dispatched to 657 East Falmouth Highway to give Melvin Reine a summons for the accident. But before the officer could rip it out of his ticket book, he got a call from the brass. Captain Paulino Rodriques told the patrol cop to back off, that because it was such a minor crime, it was a waste of police resources.

The patrol cop was puzzled and kept a copy of the citation just in case someone tried to jam him up later for not issuing it. It was not a minor crime to rear-end a marked police cruiser, especially given that there was a detective-captain behind the wheel. It was considered by most of the cops on the Falmouth police force a major middle finger thrown up to the cops—once again—by the Falmouth Fox, especially given that the cop driving the cruiser had a blood connection to the attacker. To this day, the Falmouth police force cannot present a copy of an accident report that stemmed from the 1983 incident. There is no record of the threats Melvin Reine reportedly screeched—"I'll kill you! I'll kill you!"—as he slammed Shirley's Volkswagen into the cruiser at top speed.

Melvin Reine was never issued a citation, but there was paperwork regarding a check for $356 that was written to the town to pay for the damage to the cruiser.

In other towns, that would certainly be a hefty criminal charge. But Rodriques, the police chief, may have been compromised by a personal relationship with Melvin Reine. It seemed that the Falmouth Fox had his hooks in everyone who lived in the town. His relationship with the police chief went way, way back.

Rodriques lived roughly a half-mile from the Reine compound and had been a Falmouth cop since 1962. In addition, Rodriques ran a Mickey Mouse auto body shop, a place where he could work on his own cars and maybe tinker on the cars of his friends. One afternoon he was using an acetylene torch for a welding project when the flames ignited the gas tank. There was a massive blast that could be heard for nearly a mile. Rodriques was badly burned. There was no one around as he writhed in pain. Then he felt the hands of his neighbor Melvin Reine lead him out of the flames. It was the Falmouth Fox who rushed the injured cop to the hospital in his own personal vehicle. For once, Melvin Reine was credited with doing something good for a cop. But apparently, Rodriques felt like he owed Melvin Reine for the rest of his life.

Rodriques was the captain who decided that it was not worth citing Reine for rear-ending Skip Medeiros. Rodriques' brother-in-law, also a cop on the Falmouth force, had been accused of giving Busby's work schedule to Reine in the days leading up to the shooting. That cop, Arthur "Monty" Monteiro (who has since died), was paid to help Reine expand the garage that housed trash trucks for Five Star Enterprises. He was also spotted socializing with Reine more than once.

Despite its many good, dedicated cops, the Falmouth Police Department was still painted with the same blanket indictment of ineptitude when it came to Melvin Reine. And why wouldn't they be? Melvin Reine was able to beat any number of raps and to threaten cops with abandon. Melvin Reine was able to take over the town for decades, because even the good police officers did not have the support they needed from commanding officers. As a result, Falmouth cops were threatened, harassed and forced to quash criminal cases against Reine.

John Busby was not the first cop who actually suffered a bullet after he took on "the local gunslinger," as Todd Reine told policemen. There were others who had very nearly been taken out by the Falmouth Fox or were forced to live in fear after there were threats made. Those threats were taken a bit more seriously after Busby's face was blown off. Even the toughest cops had to worry about their families; had to worry about their personal property being torched. Melvin Reine had done it in the past.

Fred Bohnenberger was the first to report to his superiors that Melvin Reine had asked him, "Do you smell smoke?" That threat came back in 1968. In 1979 Reine was apparently brazen enough to try to kill John Busby after he pulled a KKK-style hood over his head and squeezed off three pellets from a pump-action shotgun. Then in 1983 Reine rammed Medeiros' cruiser. Around that same time, Reine tried to take on Fred Bohnenberger's son, Kris, who had followed his father onto the Falmouth police force. Kris Bohnenberger, who is now a state trooper on Cape Cod, hated the way Reine was coddled, and had remembered his late father talking about what a creep Melvin Reine was. Kris, like his father, was not a man easily intimidated.

Massachusetts required diesel trucks to pay taxes on their loads. Bohnenberger had stopped Melvin Reine because he did not have the proper tax stamps on Five Star Enterprises' trucks. The fines were hefty, $250 for each one. Before Bohnenberger could even write up the paperwork, he received a phone call from Chief Rodriques. The request from his commander was stunning. He wanted Kris Bohnenberger to give Melvin Reine a break, and implied that he was to back off the Falmouth Fox.

"Rodriques wanted me to give Melvin a thirty-day grace period," Bohnenberger would remember. "What the chief didn't know is that I had seen Melvin show up at his house. He let him in. I couldn't believe he allowed Melvin Reine into his house. What kind of police commander lets the local gangster into his home? Into his home with his wife, with his family? I would never do it, and I was surprised that Chief Rodriques did."

Bohnenberger refused to give Reine the grace period—much to the chagrin of his boss, who would later exact payback by not backing him after an accusation of police brutality. Bohnenberger would be convicted of using excessive force in Falmouth, a conviction that was later overturned. He decided it was a good time to leave the Falmouth police, and became a Massachusetts State Trooper, a job he enjoys today. He lives with his wife Jen and their children in a waterfront house in Mashpee, and feels grateful to be alive.

"Melvin Reine threatened my father. He shot Busby over a traffic violation. Then he tried to kill me," Bohnenberger alleges. "I'm just glad he wasn't able to carry out his plan. I was never worried about him coming after me, it's my family that I was always concerned about."

The plan that Melvin Reine hatched against Bohnenberger involved paying a local heroin addict and petty crook to shoot the cop. Bohnenberger was an active cop, was one of those guys who kicked in doors and busted drug dealers. One afternoon he gave chase to a Falmouth junkie. As they wrestled on the ground, the addict snarled to Bohnenberger, "I shoulda shot ya like Melvin wanted." Then he shut up.

It was not until the following morning when Bohnenberger, along with officers Brian Dunne and Phil Furtado, escorted the addict into court that he got the whole story about the intended assassination attempt against him.

"Kris, you've always been fair to me. I have something to tell you. Be careful of that Falmouth Fox, that Melvin Reine. He wants something bad to happen to you. He tried to get me to shoot you," the suspect said. Then he made it clear that he would not testify against Melvin Reine. He also said he would deny he had ever uttered those words.

"He was scared of Melvin—everyone was," said Bohnenberger. He remembered being enraged because he had a wife and kids. Again he reiterated the ire that the crusaders like his dad had always felt about the John Busby shooting and the lack of action that was taken against Melvin Reine at the time. "John Busby was shot for a traffic ticket. He almost died, and now Melvin was trying get some local riff-raff to shoot me?"

Of course Bohnenberger wrote up a report and filed it with his Falmouth police superiors. But in typical fashion, the investigation went nowhere.

But in 1984, Melvin Reine would learn it would not be as easy to thwart a state police investigation. For decades he had operated his personal life and his businesses with one motto: laws did not apply to him. No rules did. As a result, he was becoming a very rich man and his businesses had burgeoned into a multi-million dollar empire. Five Star Enterprises had trash-hauling contracts all over Cape Cod, from Falmouth to the very tip of Massachusetts in Wellfleet and Provincetown. Reine was the go-to guy for any business owner who needed to get rid of trash. Making money did not stop him from trying to manipulate the system. The way trash-hauling worked is that the businesses paid Reine to empty their Dumpsters, and Reine paid the town dumps to get rid of the garbage. Reine, however, decided there could be more money made if he didn't have to pay to dump his hauls. He had a key to the gate of the landfill that comprised the Falmouth Town Dump—why not use it? Who would notice a few extra piles of garbage hauled in from Yarmouth and Cotuit and Hyannis?

Well, town officials noticed in the early 1980s, but no one seemed to have the guts to do anything about it until the state police got involved. There was one public works commissioner, a newcomer to Falmouth, who had heard that Melvin Reine from Five Star Enterprises had a key to the landfill. That Commissioner, Virginia Valieila, told police officers her suspicions, but no one took her seriously. Then she told other Falmouth town officials, but nothing was done. She later said she'd taken matters into her own hands and watched the landfill from her car late one night. Sure enough, a Five Star Enterprises truck pulled up to the gate, opened it with a key and dumped its haul inside. There was a search of the trash left there, and mail addressed to other towns confirmed that Melvin Reine was using Falmouth's landfill to avoid paying to dump his hauls in the appropriate towns. She had the proof, and she wanted something done. She wanted someone to retrieve the key from him—but no one would. They were terrified to ask the Falmouth Fox.

"The fact that he would burn things down would really scare people. Nobody wanted to cross him," Valieila told a reporter from the *Cape Cod Times*. Instead, town officials changed the locks and built a special fence to stop the after-hours dumping in 1982. Valieila was startled that the entire town could be so fearful of a single man. "I'd call it a chronic problem [the] town had that they didn't know how to deal with, even though they knew it wasn't right."

Two years after Falmouth bilked its taxpayers for the cost of a new fence around the landfill, and failed to bill the person who'd caused them to change the landfill locks, the state police would move in on Melvin Reine—finally. In 1984, state troopers arrested Reine and his then partner in Five Star Enterprises, a businessman named Charles Cacciola. The two men were accused of rigging bids to make sure they still got the contracts to haul the town's trash—not just commercial trash, but the pickup for the entire town. Selectmen did not have the guts to pull Five Star Enterprises' contract even after the public works commissioner's investigation proved that Reine was stealing from the town.

How it worked, state police said, was that Reine and Cacciola worked in collusion with another trash company, B&M Disposal, to get the bid. The Five Star Enterprises company heads wanted B&M Disposal to put in a ridiculously high bid, and then Reine and Cacciola could undercut them with a smaller bid. Or, even easier, B&M Disposal could back out of the bid entirely and force Falmouth to hire Five Star Enterprises. Of course, B&M Disposal could expect a fat kickback for their cooperation. It was an old game, one that had been used by New York City's five crime families for decades until they were crushed by that state's then–Attorney General Rudolph Giuliani. Falmouth would be strong-armed into continuing to do business with Melvin Reine because his bid to haul the garbage came in thousands of dollars below the one by his competitor. B&M would not be targeted by an arsonist. They might even make a little bit of money. Everyone would be happy. At least that's what the Falmouth Fox thought.

But the folks at B&M Disposal were tired of getting bilked by a scumbag like Melvin Reine. They were a legitimate outfit, and they were not going to be intimidated by a small-time wannabe gangster. One of B&M's officials agreed to wear a wire. Maybe the state police could finally put Melvin Reine and Five Star Enterprises completely out of business.

It almost worked. Cacciola had never been arrested before, and he panicked when he heard the litany of charges against him: conspiracy, attempt to commit a crime, perjury, collusive bidding. He was not a tough guy. He had no desire to go to jail. He could not believe that he'd gotten pulled into a criminal conspiracy, even though people had warned him about Melvin Reine. In the end, Cacciola decided he was not going to prison, and agreed to testify against Melvin Reine. The plan backfired.

Melvin Reine went to trial and was found not guilty by a jury of his peers. It was an astonishing verdict to the state troopers who spent years trying to take Reine down, thinking if they got him on this crime he might spill his guts on some of the more serious unsolved crimes. Cape and Islands District Attorney's Office prosecutors presented evidence that included testimony not just from Cacciola, but from B&M Disposal heads who testified that Reine fully intended to steal from Falmouth and rig the bidding process. It was a serious crime, one that could have resulted in federal racketeering charges. The jury was not moved by the testimony. After all, it was a jury comprised of folks from Falmouth, fully aware who Melvin Reine was. Maybe one or two of them did not relish the possibility that they might "smell smoke" upon their return from convicting Reine. Whatever the reason, they found Reine not guilty. He walked out of court that 1984 day with a grin across his face.

Cacciola's cooperation agreement did not carry much weight with state prosecutors or with a jury. He was convicted of bid rigging in 1984. Now a convicted felon, Cacciola was grateful that his sentence was just probation. But his business was destroyed, his personal finances were in ruins and he had to report to a probation officer. It was incredibly embarrassing for a guy like him to be a convict in a small town like Falmouth. Cacciola had never been arrested in his life, and barely had a traffic violation on his record. Melvin Reine was a crook and an arsonist with rumors that he'd killed at least one person and made two others disappear. If the humiliation was not enough, he also had to live with the fact that his criminal cohort had been acquitted of all charges by a jury. *He gets off and I'm convicted?*

If investigators were surprised that Reine got off, they were stunned that he then continued to be awarded lucrative contracts to haul Falmouth's trash. It was a staggering slap in the face to other business owners and to the cops who worked hard trying to take him down.

It would not take long for Melvin Reine to figure out another way to beat the system. If he couldn't break into the Falmouth landfill, he would simply steal a 10-acre parcel of family property along the Backus River in East Falmouth that had been left to him and his three siblings, and start burying trash there. Who knows when he decided that would be a solution to his dumping problems? But when the state's Environmental Protection Agency finally caught up to the scheme in the early 1990s, the parcel had become a hazardous waste site, a problem that would take decades and hundreds of thousands of dollars to clean up. It was a danger to the public and had probably polluted the waters of the nearby river. To this day, many people wonder if it was the Reine boys who dropped a dime about the waste site to the state agencies. They'd been feuding with their father over the business then, and wanted to send him a message. That message was that they could manipulate the system just as they had watched him do for decades.

The state's investigation of the dump site created even more chaos on the Reine compound. Melvin and his wife Shirley Reine went to Falmouth Town Hall and got copies of deeds for the Old Barnstable Road property. The deeds showed that Melvin and Shirley Reine owned 100 percent of the property with no mention of its rightful owners, which included John Reine and their sister. Even though the property had essentially been stolen from Melvin's siblings, a judge ruled that they were responsible for helping pay for the cleanup.

Even if it was unclear what provoked the attorney general's office and the Environmental Protection Agency to search the site, it was clear that Todd Reine and his older brother Melvin Jr. used the dump as yet another bargaining chip in their fight with Shirley Reine over Five Star Enterprises, which had been signed over to her. Investigators who showed up at the site were disgusted at how much debris had been allowed to accumulate on it without town officials noticing, or caring. The ground was littered with destruction and demolition surplus. There were abandoned cars and appliances, home heating oil tanks and paint cans, toxic fluids and auto parts buried forty feet below the dirt spreading out over half the property. There were even Five Star Enterprises garbage bins protruding from the dirt, buried underground with rotting, stinking trash.

After receiving the tip back in 1999 that the Reine-owned site was a disaster area and posed a threat to the river water, the attorney general's office stepped in. The lawyer who handled the case for the state, Paul Molloy, was not taking any chances with the Falmouth Fox. He had heard the snide comments that Melvin Reine would get away with the landfill just like he got away with everything else. He had seen Reine's rap sheet. Molloy did not have any choice but to try to keep the investigation into the property as quiet as possible.

He wrote a letter to the town of Falmouth asking officials to butt out of the state's case and leave the matter entirely in the hands of the attorney general's office. The town took the matter up for discussion and Falmouth Town Counsel Frank K. Duffy discussed the state's request in an internal town memo:

> There is a potential for execution of an environmental search warrant that would include significant excavation and/or sampling in the immediate future. He voiced concern that in the past Mr. Reine has learned of the intentions of law enforcement and that he has been able to thwart similar efforts with such advanced knowledge.

So, even state officials who worked out of a building in downtown Boston, 100 miles away from Falmouth, knew that similar law enforcement investigations into Reine had been squelched.

Duffy was furious and began to lead the charge that Falmouth town officials should sue, and sue everyone who owned a piece of the property: Reine; his brothers and sisters, who were also listed as land owners; and Shirley because she was running Five Star Enterprises.

As that investigation made its way through the painfully slow civil process in Massachusetts, Melvin Reine was arrested again.

This time the year was 1999 and he was the one charged with assault and battery on a police officer, threatening to commit murder, reckless driving, resisting arrest and disorderly conduct. In that case a Falmouth police officer named Ruben Ferrer tried to stop Reine from speeding. Reine refused to pull over, took off and led the cop on a high-speed chase. When he was cornered, Reine tried to run the officer over. No one could make those serious charges disappear, but someone could certainly get to a jury. Despite the evidence against Reine and the testimony of the cop who had nearly been run down, the Falmouth Fox was found not guilty at trial.

Despite that stunning verdict, the case still had financial ramifications for Shirley Reine and her husband's siblings. All of the Reines named on the deed were responsible for the cleanup, but Shirley took over the mission. In return, she wanted to run the trash business without interference from her stepsons or her brother-in-law. John Reine acquiesced; the boys did not. By then, her husband's mind had begun to deteriorate and he started his slide into insanity. It was becoming harder and harder for Shirley to keep Five Star Enterprises afloat as the company had fines levied against it, and was obliged to pay for the expensive cleanup of the Old Barnstable property. She started to complain loudly, especially in the press, that Falmouth officials were "making it sound much worse than it is." The *Cape Cod Times* was reporting on the dump site with increasing frequency. People in town were giving Shirley Reine the same sort of dirty looks that Melvin Reine's first wife used to receive when he'd been sent away for those arsons decades earlier.

Things were bad in Falmouth for Shirley Reine. Still, she had no idea how bad they were about to get.

FOURTEEN

Todd Reine climbed out of a green trash truck. He was wearing khaki pants and a greasy green T-shirt. The underarms of his shirt were stained with sweat. His raven-black hair was tousled and he looked as if he had not seen a toothbrush in a couple of days. Despite his dirty appearance, Reine was undeniably charming. He had not inherited his father's strange, distant stare, but instead looked directly in the eyes of anyone he was speaking to. He was a father now and wanted people to think that he was productive member of society. In order to do that, he wanted to set the record straight with a reporter.

On a sweltering hot afternoon, Reine pulled into a secluded parking lot in Plymouth, Massachusetts—the first town "off Cape" and a safe place to meet without the prying eyes of nosy neighbors. Todd Reine wanted to talk about his mother, Wanda, a woman he barely remembered now that he was in his late thirties. She had been gone since he was 4.

He flipped down the visor of the trash truck and presented an aging color photo of Wanda taken just months before she'd left her house with Todd's dad and never returned. She was wearing her trademark tortoiseshell eyeglasses and had a gentle smile spread across her face. She was always smiling when her boys were close by, and in the photograph, she had both of them on her lap. It was clear that the woman in the photograph loved her children. The boys looked at her adoringly as well. The picture was all Todd had left of Wanda.

"All I'm looking for is answers. What happened to my mother," Todd said, and glanced down at her face to really drive the point home. "I'm not trying to hurt anyone else in my family. I just want to know what happened to my mother."

Word around Falmouth was that Todd was the most like his father. Charming and gregarious until you crossed him. And you knew you had crossed him when you saw his brown eyes go dead.

His stepmother Shirley had crossed him. Todd Reine wanted to talk about Shirley too that summer afternoon. How she was no good. How she had taken advantage of his father. How she was running his inheritance into the ground. His brother Melvin's inheritance. Both of the boys now had children of their own. They didn't want to hurt Shirley. But they had to protect what was rightfully theirs, and in the minds of Todd and Melvin Jr., they only had one recourse to make sure they could do just that: sue their stepmother.

Todd continued to talk. It was almost as if he did not care who he was talking to. It was a speech more than a conversation. He ranted about his father being sent to a loony bin. He pointed out that Shirley had taken to running around with his father's criminal cohorts. He spoke about the loaded gun found in a diaper bag in Shirley's house. But the story started, as so many did in Falmouth, with the criminal antics of Melvin Reine.

Todd said that his relationship with his father was damaged beyond repair in 1999 when "it was very clear to me that my father was having serious mental problems." That was also the year that Melvin Reine threw his sons out of the family business. Todd's relationship with his father was strained, but Melvin Reine had a soft spot for his grandchildren. He would show up to watch his grandson, Todd's boy, play baseball. But unfortunately, his behavior would be a distraction to everyone else trying to take in the Little League game. The Falmouth Fox would be known to pull alongside the field in his truck and blare the stereo and lean on the truck's air horn for no apparent reason but to create a scene. Shirley would race to the driver's door and plead with her husband to cut the noise. His grandson would be horrified. And Todd could not decide initially if his father was losing it or intentionally trying to push his buttons. Todd decided that he would try to spend time with his father and get over the argument about the family business. Those visits would leave him concerned about his father's health. Melvin Reine was never a friendly guy or fond of small talk, but he always held his own—especially if the topic turned to the old days and criminal behavior. Then you couldn't shut him up. But these days Todd noted that his dad's conversations were erratic, with Melvin jumping from topic to topic.

He'd always been a volatile guy, but Melvin was now snapping at his grandchildren, which was unlike him.

Those mental problems escalated on a crisp fall day in 2001. Melvin Reine was still driving for his trash-hauling business, and went to pick up a container behind a local corner store called Kenyon's Market. A woman had pulled in with a moving truck to pick up a few things for the summer cottage she was going to move into that weekend, and blocked access to the Dumpster. She could not have been in the small store for more than a few minutes, but Melvin Reine did not want to wait.

He flew into a rage. People inside the store heard an explosive crunch and looked outside. Reine had used the lifts on the trash truck to ram into the woman's moving van, and had started to heave it off the ground with all of her belongings inside. The woman pleaded with him to stop and jumped behind the wheel to try to prevent Reine from causing any more damage to the rental vehicle—or her belongings.

"What are you doing?" she screamed at him. "I would have moved it. Why did you have to do this?"

"Bitch, I will get a shotgun and blow your head off," Reine snarled to her. Then he proceeded to try to smash her rental truck's windshield with the forks of his truck.

Police were called. It was October 2001. The nation was still reeling from the September 11 terror attacks. It was a different time for the nation, and a different time in Falmouth. Reine's problem solvers on the police force had retired or moved on to better jobs. The Falmouth Fox did not have juice with the local cops anymore. The rookies knew Reine had a reputation as a tough guy, but to them he just looked like a broken-down old man, a smelly one at that.

Melvin Reine was arrested at the scene and arraigned the next day at Falmouth District Court on charges of assault and battery with a dangerous weapon, malicious destruction of property over $250, and threatening to commit murder. While out on bail, his mental problems escalated. A neighbor pissed him off, so he dumped a load of garbage on her lawn. He would curse out loud to no one in particular. All he had to do was swath himself in a dirty bathrobe and his behavior would be identical to the antics pulled off by one of his criminal heroes: Vincent "The Chin" Gigante.

On November 29, 2001, Melvin Reine had a pretrial hearing at Falmouth District Court. It was brief but tedious. He listened to a lecture about how he had to stay out of trouble. For some reason, hours after his case had already been heard and his attorney had vacated the building, the Falmouth Fox returned. He was fuming, and tried to rush the bench of Judge Don Carpenter.

"I want to talk to you," Reine yelled at the judge. The outburst disrupted the court's afternoon proceedings. Petty criminals and wife beaters stared. Prosecutors and defense attorneys did not pay Reine much attention. They were used to Melvin Reine around the Falmouth courthouse.

"We need to talk!" Reine continued. "I want answers! I want pillows! This is unacceptable!" He ranted about pillows on the chairs in the courthouse and other nonsense. He thought it appalling that the pews in the courthouse were so uncomfortable, and demanded change.

Reine was so angry, spittle flew from his mouth. Judge Carpenter ordered that he be removed from the court and undergo a ten-day psychiatric evaluation. The order called for Melvin Reine to be hospitalized to protect himself and the public from his bizarre and volatile behavior. Once he arrived at the Taunton State Hospital, where there is a unit for the criminally insane, Reine was assessed by a psychologist in the Court Clinic program administered by the University of Massachusetts Medical School Forensic Health Services Department. A report was written up that would become part of Reine's criminal file. Of course, the first thing noted on the report was the fact that Reine had no medical insurance or primary care physician. He was a millionaire who had never bothered to buy a health insurance policy for himself or his wife, Shirley.

Melvin Reine's psychological evaluation was conducted by a doctor named Nancy Connolly. In her report she wrote:

> *Mr. Reine was evaluated today after an incident in the courtroom where Mr. Reine approached the judge's bench and would not step back when told to do so. Mr. Reine explained to me that he wanted to speak to the judge about providing cushions for the seats in the courtroom. He wanted to have a personal discussion with the judge. Earlier in the day, he had a clerk's hearing at the courthouse but had no business pending in the courtroom. Mr. Reine's mental state was reportedly deteriorating and he had been observed by his attorney and others in the court (Reportedly, he testified in another case and he did not do well). His wife recently brought him to a doctor to R/O Alzheimer's. He was prescribed Aricept but is not taking it. There have been noticeable memory problems and confusion for 1–2 years. Mr. Reine has demonstrated behavioral changes according to his wife. One example was he dumped a load of trash onto someone's lawn for no apparent reason. Mr. Reine had no hx [history] of psycho treatment and no hx of drug/alcohol abuse. He has a significant criminal record for past violence.*

Dr. Connolly went on to note that Reine owned his own business, and his education had ended with the seventh grade. "He is smiling inappropriately, oriented to person, place but not time. Patient is very confused. Tangential. Rambling responses," Connolly wrote next to a category on her intake sheet marked *Behavioral observations/alertness/orientation.*

Connolly had no way of knowing that smiling inappropriately was commonplace for the Falmouth Fox. So was rambling.

Next to a question about *mood/affect*, Connolly wrote: "good." She said that Melvin told her, "I help a lot of people."

Connolly stated that Melvin Reine began to ramble about "helping people, saving people."

Then in the category labeled *Thought process/thought content*, Connolly wrote that Reine was:

> *confused, delusional. Patient thinks he has kidney cancer. He has been delusional for past 1–2 years. Patient reported "hearing voices" and said:*
>   *"Yes, I hear them talking. Talking about boats."*

The intake form asked if Melvin Reine was suicidal or homicidal and Connolly wrote: "Patient denied past violence," but noted that "he has a past criminal record including arson."

Then came a section for Connolly's opinion on Reine's state of mind regarding his competence to stand trial and/or criminal responsibility. She wrote:

> *Mr. Reine did not seem to understand about the warnings. He thought I was talking to him about his medication. Even after I repeated statements that I was evaluating him for the court, he continued to think that evaluation related to his medication. Mr. Reine could not identify any charges he had in court. Even when I told him he was charged with threatening to commit a crime, he could not remember any charges. Mr. Reine explained he approached the judge to discuss putting cushions on the chairs in the court (no criminal charges for the courtroom incident). When asked if he thought it was okay to approach the judge*

*he gave a rambling response about always helping
people. He talked about saving a lot of people, including the police chief in Falmouth. Mr. Reine had a
vague understanding of his attorney's role—"he does
a good job," Mr. Reine said. He did not know the role
of the prosecutor. He thought the judge was "a nice
man" and "the boss" but he did not seem to grasp
much about the adversarial nature of the proceedings. He rambled about people getting lung cancer
and unrelated material.*

Then came Connolly's recommendations:

*In my opinion, Mr. Reine's mental functioning is
significantly impaired, possible due to organic causes,
although not known. He has no known history of mental illness.*

She ordered that Reine undergo further evaluation at Taunton State Hospital's facility for the criminally insane. He was
admitted that afternoon—and would never leave the hospital again.

If Melvin Reine had planned his hospitalization as a way
to manipulate the system and avoid criminal prosecution, it
worked. He was still crafty as ever. As a result of his hospitalization, the assault and battery case against Reine for
threatening to blow off a tourist's head with a shotgun was
dismissed. The expensive cleanup of the Old Barnstable
landfill that Melvin Reine had turned into a hazardous waste
site was left to his wife and siblings, who'd had nothing to
do with the construction debris and reeking garbage that
had been dumped there.

In July 2001, after his arrest, Melvin Reine signed over
his entire life to Shirley. In the power of attorney document,
she would take care of all of his business affairs and make
all the decisions—a headache, really. But when Melvin
Reine finally died, she would inherit everything. The business. The house. All of his assets. His sons were written out

of the will. So were his grandkids. To any prosecutors who might hope to bring Melvin Reine up on charges in connection with the crimes that his sons and brother were now spilling their guts about, the power of attorney document made it clear that he was insane and could not be held responsible for his actions anymore.

In the words of his attorney, Frederick Mycock, Melvin Reine was "beyond prosecution in any state."

"We're not having any trials," Mycock told reporters who asked him how Reine would answer to the charges that he'd illegally dumped materials at his Old Barnstable Road property. "He can't be questioned. He couldn't understand his rights."

Reine had had no history of psychiatric problems, and had begun to unravel publicly at a very convenient time. Maybe he did have dementia. Maybe he didn't. One thing was certain though: Reine's attorney was right. There would be no trials for Reine's crime sprees. In April 2002, a Falmouth judge heard testimony from Reine's attorney that he was not competent to stand trial.

Shirley was the only relative in the courtroom to support Melvin Reine during the hearing. She was wearing a simple sweater and a pair of eyeglasses as she listened to the testimony about her husband. Her looks had been zapped from her. Her hair was dry and limp, her fingernails ragged and colorless. Gone was the sexpot who had mesmerized the Falmouth Fox as a teenager. She was a beaten-down housewife now, with a world of problems.

It had been six months since Melvin Reine was sent for the initial psychological evaluation. During that time, he convinced doctors that he was "mentally ill and incompetent." Taunton State Hospital forensic psychologist Dr. Charles N. Moore took the stand. He described how he'd come to believe that Melvin Reine suffered from a progressive form of dementia that had left him confused without memory.

"He is more and more withdrawn and he won't look at or respond to the staff, even when asked repeatedly to acknowledge them," Moore testified. "Mr. Reine won't eat anything unless it is brought to him by his wife. He keeps his room neat, but he won't shower or shave unless prompted by his wife or staff. He looks very blank, staring into space.

"He spends a lot of time in bed waiting for his wife to visit. He doesn't interact with any staff or peers," Moore testified. He also said that Reine was increasingly agitated. "He's quite threatening and vulgar when he is angry. He's unpredictable. He's a very unhappy man."

Moore also said that the Falmouth Fox was up to his old criminal tricks. Perhaps the cuckoo act had been real—or was becoming real, the result of spending so much time around insane people. Melvin Reine had tried to bribe staffers with a promise of a BMW if they helped him escape the nuthouse. It was a promise he could not follow through with, of course, because Shirley controlled the purse strings now. But he tried to get staffers to open the door and spring him nonetheless, Moore said.

Reine also talked about the day he would leave and drive his trucks again, another delusion that was indicative of his dementia. Then there was the arrogance and the outright dismissal of authority that Reine had shown throughout his life, long before he was sent to a hospital for the criminally insane. If there was a fire drill at the hospital, Melvin Reine would lock himself in his room and refuse to leave, causing a skirmish with the staff. He once locked himself in a bathroom with a razor blade when he could not get what he wanted for dinner. There were the usual scowls and threats and intimidation tactics that had served him so well throughout his life, but did not have a lot of effect with people who worked in a locked ward with a lot of nut cases. He tried to talk about "smelling smoke" and "dropping a dime," but those taunts did not mean anything to a tired hospital staffer who could simply order Reine back to his room and lock him in from the outside.

"In my opinion," Moore testified, "he still has the ability to assault. If released, he poses substantial risk to himself or others."

Reine's attorney Frederick Mycock argued that afternoon

that his client should be moved from Taunton State Hospital into a more pleasurable setting, at the taxpayers' expense, of course. There was an assisted-living facility in Centerville, not far from the water. Certainly the Falmouth Fox, with his failing health, could benefit from high-thread-count cotton sheets and sitting on a the porch of a nice facility where his black hair could be blown back by soothing sea breezes.

When the judge raised an eyebrow at Mycock's suggestion, the lawyer pointed out that the Centerville facility had locked doors too, but it also had some nice perks. Visitors' hours were more lenient and the food was much better. Sure, it would be expensive and Reine did not have health insurance, but that was something that could be worked out financially between the state of Massachusetts and Melvin Reine's estate keeper, Shirley.

Mycock then put his own expert witness on the stand. Dr. Gerald Elovitz testified that Reine had frontal lobe dementia that was growing worse with each passing day. Elovitz also declared that Reine had an IQ of 50, which was equivalent to a form of mild retardation. It would not be fair to keep a man whose IQ was so low in a hospital where he shared space with violent and truly insane criminals. For Melvin Reine's health and state of mind, he should be moved to a private hospital, Elovitz said.

Judge Michael Creedon oversaw the hearing into Reine's state of mind, and had been familiar with the long history of the Falmouth Fox for decades. To appease Mycock, the judge said he would consider the pricey assisted-living facility, but mused out loud that it was unlikely to be an appropriate setting for Melvin Reine.

"I know Melvin Reine. I've seen the outbursts in court. There's something to see," Creedon said from the bench during the proceedings. "My biggest concern is that he would wander off and get into trouble."

Trouble that could lead to someone's house being burned to the ground. Trouble that could lead to an unexplained disappearance. Trouble that could bring crime-scene investigators to the area near the Reine compound to fish a body out of the cranberry bog was the fear on the minds of many.

Creedon decided that Taunton State Hospital was the best place to keep Melvin Reine confined. Shirley Reine had paperwork drawn up that made her the trustee of her husband's estate. With that, Melvin signed everything over to Shirley Reine. Five Star Enterprises. His property. All of his assets. Anything and everything relating to the business. The boys were written out completely. So were his siblings. Shirley got it all.

Melvin Jr. and Todd were not going to take that lying down. They had put up with their father for a very long time and the Falmouth Fox owed them. In short order, the boys filed a lawsuit against their stepmother. But legal action alone wasn't enough for Todd Reine, who began to cooperate with Falmouth police officers against Shirley. He told cops about a gun she had on her property, along with equipment his father had stolen from other worksites. He talked about the Busby shooting and his father's illicit relationship with some Falmouth police officers. Todd Reine's cooperation would lead to a raid on Shirley's house a year after his father had been put away.

Todd was all too happy to describe that raid in detail as he leaned against his own trash truck that summer afternoon in a Plymouth parking lot. As he talked, he would borrow a line that had been uttered by a longtime family friend.

"Shirley was no Cinderella," Todd said, shaking his head. "Believe me. She had an evil side."

So, apparently, did Todd Reine.

FIFTEEN

Todd Reine's harassment of his stepmother would not stop with the civil lawsuit he and his brother filed against her. He would hound his Uncle John to tell cops what he knew, using every tactic he could think of. In the end, it was John Reine's own personal disgust that he was financially on the hook for the cleanup of the Old Barnstable parcel that acted as the convincer.

It was the first time John Reine would walk into the Falmouth Police Department stationhouse without wearing bracelets. This time he was not a criminal suspect, but a police informant. It was a role he never thought he would find himself filling, but he was so sick and tired of Melvin Reine by then, he didn't even feel like a rat—he felt like one of the crusaders. Detective Kent Clarkson was waiting for him. With the same tape recorder he'd used to create audio evidence and a paper trail of the Reine brothers' information, he began to prepare a new incident report that he planned to file in the box with the Busby shooting information. Just as he had with Todd and Melvin Jr., Clarkson listened first so he could pay attention to every word, then transcribed it onto a police report—the very police report that Cape and Islands District Attorney Michael O'Keefe would insist should remain secret; the report that he refused to allow John Busby to look at or to hand over to local reporters. Despite O'Keefe's efforts, the John Reine report was eventually leaked to a writer as well.

On 3-31-03 at 10:00 Mr. John Reine came to the station for an interview regarding the ongoing cases involving his brother Melvin Reine and his wife Shirley Reine and the property on Old Barnstable Road and 657 East Falmouth Highway. Present for the interview was Mr. Reine, Trooper Chris Mason from the Cape and Islands CPAC unit and Detective Kent Clarkson from the Falmouth Police Detective Division.

We began the meeting by asking Mr. Reine about the land dispute at 336 Old Barnstable Road. He stated that there really was nothing to dispute. Melvin Reine and Shirley Reine had taken it upon themselves to take the land and start to develop it when it didn't belong to them. He went on to explain that the land was in a trust naming Melvin Reine, John Reine, Manuel Reine, Nancy Andrade, and Marion Sharpe as all equal owners. The parcel was bequeathed to them by their mother Adeline Reine. Melvin and Shirley went to the town and pulled permits, installed water and other utilities on the property with no consent of any of the legal owners. Mr. Reine has since filed paperwork with the Superior Court in Barnstable blocking any further activity with the land or with the parcel at 657 East Falmouth Highway.

Mr. Reine went on to explain how Melvin Reine built two garages on the 657 East Falmouth Highway Parcel, one of them partially on his property and close to wetlands without any permits. Melvin Reine also erected a large garage at 336 Old Barnstable Road without any permits. John Reine stated that he questioned his brother on both buildings and that Melvin Reine stated: "Who's going to stop me? Too bad." John stated that he didn't understand how this could have happened. John stated that Melvin moved his bound stone. He stated that he was on the road and could not bother about him placing the building (partially on his property) because he feared Melvin "would burn my house down with my wife in it and not even care about it."

John stated that Melvin "screwed everybody." He spoke

about Melvin's two sons, Todd Reine and Melvin Reine Jr. that worked for him like "dogs" and didn't get paid for it. John stated that he assisted Melvin in the building of the large garage with the understanding that he would be able to work on his own truck in the garage but Melvin denied him access when the garage was finished.

I asked John about his relationship with Shirley. He stated that she wouldn't wave to him since the court action. He stated that he never really thought much of Shirley. He stated that his brother Manuel (Honey) has a good relationship with her and has always and still speaks to her. John stated that he went to Taunton State Hospital in an attempt to speak with his brother around Christmas but Melvin refused to see him and will only see Shirley.

I asked John about the stolen backhoe and the stolen Ford pickup from Westport and he stated that he didn't know anything about either of them. He stated that he saw the truck around the yard but he had thought that Melvin had purchased it. He stated that he didn't know of anything that Melvin Reine had buried on Old Barnstable Road. He stated that the only thing he brought to the property was empty roll-off containers for storage. He stated that Melvin was only allowed to dump two containers a day at the landfill in Bourne so he dumped the remainder at Old Barnstable Road property he thought that he later cleaned that all up.

John Reine started to speak of his brother's deteriorating mental state and the fact that he really hasn't been himself for 5–6 years. He stated that when the boys (Melvin Jr. and Todd) left the business he really went crazy. He stated that Shirley changed him for the worse also. He stated that Melvin was always malicious but had come out of Walpole State Prison a changed man and that when he got involved with Shirley he started being much worse. He reiterated that nobody ever said anything to him because they were scared.

John went on to speak about Melvin intimidating people and the fact that he wanted to be in charge. He stated that if anyone crossed him there would be repercussions. He repeated the fact that "Shirley is an evil person. She's evil, boy." John was asked about the arsons that Melvin had been involved in. He stated: "That was his thing. Burning things. That's how he would intimidate people." He stated that Melvin burned the Wood Lumber Company, a house at the end of Maravista Avenue by the water."

I (Detective Clarkson) then asked John if he knew Navajo Joe (Henry Silva). He looked at me and paused and stated, "Yeah, Navajo. Yeah. He was my buddy. We were running mates 15–20 years ago." He stated that they drove together for Stop & Shop. He stated that he hadn't spoken to Navajo in quite a few years. John stated that Navajo started drinking and got divorced and they lost touch with each other. I asked John if he had ever borrowed a shotgun from Navajo Joe. He responded:

"A shotgun? No never what would I do with a shotgun?"

I asked him again:

"You never borrowed a shotgun."

John Reine responded: "No, I borrowed a .22 but not a shotgun."

I explained to Mr. Reine that I had spent considerable time with Navajo Joe and he had explained that John had borrowed a shotgun because he was going hunting with his brother Melvin. John kept repeating "a .22" and explained that he wanted a .22 to shoot some rats around the yard. Trooper Mason explained that Mr. Silva never had a .22 and Mr. Reine had no response.

I asked Mr. Reine if he had ever been in the department over the years to speak with anyone about anything over the years. He stated, "Yeah. With Roger." I stated Roger Gonsalves? And he said, "Yeah. Roger Gonsalves. I came in to speak with him about the Busby shooting." Mr. Reine explained that Arthur Monteiro had come down to the Reine property right after the shooting and was laughing with Melvin stating to Melvin: "You shot Busby?" He stated that Monteiro and Melvin were laughing back and forth and he walked away because he didn't want any part of the conversation. Reine stated that Monteiro was giving Melvin information regarding who was working on the case and what they were doing. He stated that his younger nephew Arthur Joseph had heard the conversation so he didn't want anyone to think that he had done anything.

It was the most damning information about the Falmouth police force of the old days that investigators had heard yet. According to what John told police, not only did an officer provide Busby's work schedule to an assassin team, another Falmouth officer actually shared laughs with Melvin Reine over the fact that the officer and father of three was in critical condition at Massachusetts General Hospital. Both Detective Clarkson and State Trooper Mason had to stop themselves from exchanging angry looks. How could anyone laugh when a fellow law enforcement officer was gunned down? Especially when that officer had a wife and kids? Both men had a job to do and put aside the staggering fury that came with the recounting of that scene in order to continue the interview. By then, Officer "Monty" Monteiro had passed away. Even if they'd wanted to hold him accountable for setting up Busby, it was too late. They turned their attention back to what John Reine was saying. It was unbelievable that they were garnering a confession and had an eyewitness to the Busby assassination attempt—but it was completely useless. The statute of limitations had expired in 1989. Still, they allowed John Reine to continue to ramble about his brother's influence on the town of Falmouth and its leaders.

Mr. Reine stated that he came into the station to explain to Officer Gonsalves that neither he or his brother had anything to do with the shooting of Officer Busby. I asked Mr. Reine if anyone had spoken to him prior to that or after his appearance at the station regarding the Busby case. He stated, "No, only when I came in and spoke to Roger." In investigating this claim it was found that Mr. Reine confused Roger Gonsalves with Paul Gonsalves who was in detectives at the time. Retired Detective Paul Gonsalves was contacted and stated that Reine came in right after Officer Busby issued him the citation for operating to endanger and then came by again after Busby was shot to explain that he had nothing to do with it.

It was certainly unusual for a homicide investigator working on the case of a police officer who'd been shot not to mention to the district attorney's office that such an interview had taken place, John's investigator would later say. There was no paperwork about that encounter in the file at Clarkson's feet. It was also against protocol to interview a potential suspect in the case—after all, when Busby was shot, police officials had told the press that they were looking into Busby's recent arrests—and not file an official report of that interview. There was no report filed by Detective Gonsalves, nor was his exchange with John Reine recorded or reported for the district attorney's office. That the Busby case had been bungled was now indisputable. Trooper Mason and Detective Clarkson continued the interview.

When Mr. Reine mentioned John Busby's shooting I asked him if he thought his brother Melvin had anything to do with the shooting. He replied, "Did I?"

"No," Clarkson responded. "Your brother?"

He stated that he didn't believe that he had anything to do with it.

"Did you have a problem with John Busby?"

"I had no problem with Busby," John Reine said. "The only run-in I had with him was when the assistant district attorney was killed in a car accident in front of the Big Fisherman."

John Reine stated that Busby had stopped him in his tractor because of the accident. He stated that another officer had waved him on so he began to pass the scene when Busby was yelling at him as he passed Busby. Busby threw his clipboard at his truck. John Reine stated that he heard the bang on his truck.

"That's the only run-in I ever had with him," John Reine insisted.

I asked him if he had stopped to inquire what the problem was and why Officer Busby was upset and he stated that he had not.

I asked him if he had tried to run Officer Busby down that evening. He replied:

No, what do you think I'm nuts? I need my license to drive truck. I've got more sense than that."

Mr. Reine then went on to say that Busby was not near the truck. "He threw the clipboard at me."

I stated that isn't what he charged you with?

He stated that was what he was charged with but he didn't try and run him down. The cop also asked John whether he was slated to go to court in the days before Busby was shot for the assault and battery case the wounded officer brought against him.

"Yes."

What happened to the charges against you, Clarkson asked.

"They were dismissed I guess."

Mr. Reine stated that he never lost his license, adding again: "I think they dismissed it. I don't know why he ever said that I tried to run him down."

I asked Reine if Busby was a friendly guy and he replied:

"I didn't know him. That was the only time I ever spoke to him."

I explained to Reine that I had information regarding the shooting of Officer Busby and I had information that he was driving the vehicle the night of the shooting.

"Come on," Reine responded. "Not me. . . . You mean to tell me that Melvin did this?"

I explained to him the fact that we had interviewed several people regarding the shooting and asked him to be honest with Trooper Mason and I.

John Reine stopped talking. He slouched in his chair. He put his hands in the air. The detectives gave him a minute to compose himself. When he leaned forward and tossed his arms up, the cops knew they had him. "All right. All right," Reine said. And then he began to talk about that night. The investigators turned the tape recorder back on.

Melvin had approached him and stated that he needed him to drive for him. Mr. Reine stated that he jumped in the car and asked Melvin where they were going and he stated for John Reine to drive to Teaticket. Mr. Reine asked Melvin what vehicle they were in and he stated they were in the wagon that he had purchased from Mustafa. He stated that the wagon was light blue with wood sides and it was a Ford. Clarkson asked him what happened to the vehicle and Reine stated that they crushed the vehicle. Clarkson then wrote, "I asked him who crushed the vehicle and he didn't recall."

Reine stated that Melvin Reine got into the wagon and sat in the rear seat. He asked why he was sitting in the back seat and Melvin told him not to worry about it. John Reine stated that they got down to Sandwich Road and Melvin had told him that he had taken a light out of a vehicle and they the needed to watch for the vehicle missing the light. John Reine stated "I asked him what light" and Melvin responded; "Busby's Volkswagen, the left taillight." Melvin told him to pull out behind the vehicle with the one taillight so he did and then Melvin told him to pass the vehicle so he did and then Melvin shot. Clarkson asked John Reine how many shots and he responded with "I'm not sure. 2-3 shots."

I asked him exactly where Melvin was sitting and he stated that he was in the third seat, one of the little jump seats in the back of the car. He stated that he shot out the back window. Trooper Mason asked him how the shotgun ended up in the rear seat of the wagon and John Reine responded that Melvin had told him he needed a shotgun so he got one from Navajo Joe and gave it to him. John Reine stated that he didn't even know that Melvin had the shotgun in the wagon. He stated that he was unaware that it was Busby's car.

I asked Reine where they were parked and he stated that they were at the church (next door to Busby's former house) he stated that he asked Melvin why they were waiting there and Melvin responded: "You'll see." I asked Reine who else was in the car and he stated that Shirley Reine was in the front passenger's seat. I asked Reine how he knew when to go and he stated that Melvin told him when to go. He stated: "It was Melvin I didn't know what was going on, this was all new to me." Reine stated that after Melvin shot he asked him what the hell he was doing and he told him not to worry about it. Reine stated that Melvin told him it was Busby after he shot the shotgun.

I asked Reine what precipitated the shooting and he explained that Melvin had stated that Busby had messed with two members of the family and it was time that he paid. I asked him about another incident besides his incident with Busby and he was quick to respond:

"Oh No. The first was Clyde. Melvin's son Clyde. Not me."

John Reine stated that Clyde was the first and then his incident at the Big Fisherman (now Oysters Too). He stated that other kids that Melvin knew had run-ins with Busby also.

Trooper Mason asked Mr. Reine what route they took after they shot Busby and he explained that they continued southerly on Sandwich Road and then took a left on Route 28 and returned to Melvin's house at 657 East Falmouth Highway.

Trooper Mason asked Reine if he saw Melvin load the shotgun and he repeated that he didn't even know he had the shotgun. Trooper Mason asked him if he had received ammunition from Navajo Joe and he stated that Melvin had his own shotgun ammunition. Trooper Mason asked John how prior to the shooting did he give the shotgun to Melvin and he stated that it was approximately one week prior. I asked Reine what the shotgun looked like and he stated that he didn't recall. He stated that it was a regular shotgun.

John Reine stated that Busby was at the court all bandaged up when the charges were dismissed. Trooper Mason asked John what Shirley said in the vehicle during the shooting and he stated that she was silent. He stated that Shirley knew all about the intention to shoot Busby prior to the shooting.

I asked Reine where the car was after the shooting and he stated that the Busby car was on the side of the roadway (west side) of Sandwich Road. He stated that he saw it in his mirror and then drove home. He stated that he pulled into Melvin's yard, gave Melvin the key, and went to his house without another word.

He stated approximately two weeks later he went to Melvin's and got the shotgun from Melvin and told him he was going to return the shotgun to Navajo Joe. John Reine stated that he kept it quiet and they all stated they needed to keep it quiet because they were "looking at jail. Looking at jail."

I then asked Reine about the murder of Flanagan. He stated that Flanagan used to come around the yard all the time. He stated that the morning he saw the police going down to the bogs, he asked Melvin about the death and Melvin never said anything. He stated that Shirley was cleaning Melvin's Cadillac at her house right before they found Flanagan in the bogs.

I asked Reine why Melvin would have wanted to kill Flanagan and he stated "just to send a message." John stated that Melvin felt he was being bothered by the police and that is why he started with the fires. He stated that Melvin's quote was:

"I'll give the cops something to do."

He went on to explain some of the fires that Melvin had set.

I asked Mr. Reine about Wanda Reine and her disappearance and he stated that he didn't know anything about it. He stated that Wanda was a wonderful girl and Melvin treated her like a dog. He stated that Shirley probably knows. He stated that Melvin would tell Shirley everything and Melvin was dating Shirley when Wanda was still around. John Reine stated that Shirley was the motivation for Wanda's disappearance. John Reine stated that the day the state and Falmouth Police were digging the garage floor Melvin went in his house and Melvin had a shotgun in his possession telling John that he ought to go out and shoot all of the state troopers. John stated that he talked Melvin out of it.

I asked Reine about Alwardt and he stated that Alwardt was giving information about Melvin's arsons that he was doing and all of the sudden Alwardt disappeared. He stated that Alwardt told Mustafa (Ahmed) about him retrieving fuel oil for an arson that Melvin did and Melvin found out about it.

John stated again that if he could help us with the unsolved homicides he would but he didn't know anything about them. He stated that he thought the world of Wanda and he would help find her if he knew anything. He stated that Melvin was hooked up with some organized crime people from up north in those days. He reiterated that Shirley has information about all of the homicides in his opinion.

Despite all the evidence that had just been delivered to investigators by John Reine, it was not enough for Cape and Islands District Attorney Michael O'Keefe. The report would remain a secret, and O'Keefe had the law on his side. He declared it part of an open homicide investigation, which meant that the secretary of state's office—the only state power that could overrule a district attorney on a public records issue—would side with O'Keefe. O'Keefe had issues already in 2003. The murder of fashion writer Christa Worthington had focused a worldwide media glare on his small office after Maria Flook wrote about his towel-clad interview.

It was an embarrassing episode, to say the least, and O'Keefe could not afford any more humiliation. He was going to be slow and methodical in dealing with the Busby matter. The cop could storm a meeting of Falmouth selectmen—which he did—and testify on Beacon Hill in Boston, but nothing changed the fact that the statute of limitations in Massachusetts was ten years for assault on a police officer. There was nothing O'Keefe could do to change that. Still, Falmouth Detective Kent Clarkson wanted to make sure he had conducted a thorough interview with John Reine, and asked him to come back into the station on April 14, 2003—just a little more than two years before Shirley Reine would be found shot dead at the Reine compound.

On April 14, 2003 Trooper John Kotfila and I (Clarkson) met with John Reine in the conference room of the police department to clarify some of the statements he had made to Trooper Mason and I when he came into the station on 3-31-03. Mr. Reine arrived at the station at 9:00 and was reminded of his rights per Miranda prior to the conversation commencing.

Mr. Reine began by explaining how he believed that his brother Melvin had sabotaged his truck after the Busby shooting to keep him quiet. He stated that Melvin wanted him out of the way and had taken out a steering bolt and he was in a severe accident with his truck in Attleboro. He stated that he was watching Melvin after that. He stated that Melvin put a knife to his son's neck because he was upset with John Reine.

I began by outlining the statement that John had given to Trooper Mason and I asked him for input. He agreed to the statement as it was written and stated that it was concisely what he had depicted. I outlined his statement about the Busby shooting and he reiterated the statement that he had given the first time he was in the briefing room.

John clarified that the Busby shooting was planned because of the three incidents involving Melvin Reine's family and friends. He stated that it was the run-in at the Big Fisherman with him (John) and the run-in with Clyde Pena and another incident with another friend of Melvin's.

John went on to explain that he witnessed Melvin Reine threatening the former Chief of Police in Falmouth, John Ferreira at the gas station where Johnnies Tune and Lube is presently. John stated that it was during the time when the state police excavated his garage floor in search of his missing wife. He (Johnnie) stated that Melvin was in the chief's face and waving his finger at him (Chief Ferreira.)

John explained that when Melvin got out of Walpole state prison he was "running" with some people that he met inside that were affiliated with the Patriarca Crime Family in Boston and that Melvin had met Patriarca. He stated that one of the people was named [withheld]. He explained how [another gangster] still is at the property occasionally meeting with Shirley.

John began to explain more about the John Busby shooting and how when John looked in the mirror prior to Melvin firing the gun he observed Melvin with a hood over his head with the eyes cut out "like the clan" as he described. He stated that Melvin meant to kill Busby but he believed that the hood twisted a little bit and caused Melvin's vision to be slightly blocked. He stated that Melvin was a perfect shot. He explained how the former director of Natural Resources used to come down to the Reine property and give Melvin his sidearm and Melvin would set up cans and his bullets hit every one, every time without missing.

He spoke about his conversation after the incident with Melvin about the shooting. He explained how he was nervous and Melvin told him if he kept his mouth shut there was nothing to worry about. Melvin explained that he and Shirley would never say anything. John stated that Melvin had the whole plan laid out prior to them going to the church to wait for Officer Busby.

John stated that after the shooting they had conversation about the shooting and he stated that Melvin implied that he better not say anything. He stated that he didn't actually threaten him but he understood not to say anything. He (John) stated that he was very nervous when he brought the gun back to Navajo Joe and he placed it in his sleeper in the bunk and returned it to Navajo Joe. He explained that he would have told the facts regarding the shooting when it occurred but was never pursued by law enforcement.

That's right. John Reine was never pursued by law enforcement and neither was his brother Melvin. It was a pattern in Falmouth. Everyone, it seemed, including hard-edged Falmouth police officers and their commanders, were afraid of the Falmouth Fox and what he could and would do. Even his own brother said out loud: "If you crossed Melvin, there would be repercussions."

No one was safe, not even Melvin's blood, his closest loved ones: Wanda was gone, and John Reine had almost been wiped out after his brother pulled a steering bolt out of his vehicle. The Falmouth Fox had been arrested more than two dozen times, but would only be convicted once back in 1968. Even then, he served a minuscule portion of his sentence for setting fires across Falmouth. He'd destroyed homes, put firefighters' lives in danger, threatened investigators in the case and served less than two years in prison. Those two dozen criminal charges Reine did accrue only came from cops brave enough to put him in bracelets. Considering how many times cops looked the other way when Reine got in trouble, it was amazing that those many charges had been logged on his criminal history.

But Shirley Reine would not be so lucky. The information that the boys revealed on their stepmother would lead to a raid on the Reine compound. The boys were not afraid to get their stepmother in trouble now that their father was in prison. He could not take action against them from a locked ward. Shirley was living all alone in that big house where Todd and Melvin Jr. had been raised.

And in that house, Shirley had a bull's-eye on her back.

SIXTEEN

August 2002 brought weather that was ungodly hot, and Shirley Reine was tired of sweating. Tired of making the two-hour round trip to Taunton State Hospital to visit Melvin. Tired of fighting with her next-door neighbor and brother-in-law John Reine. Tired of the depositions she had been forced to give after Melly and Todd filed that civil lawsuit against her. Tired of running Five Star Enterprises alone. Tired of dealing with the restaurant owners and small store franchises who complained that the trash pickups were late. Tired of the landfill cleanup headache. Tired of the dirty looks she got from Falmouth townspeople, who looked up at the gilded fox perched on the top of her house and thought her of husband. Tired of paying the bills alone. Eating alone. Living alone.

Running Five Star Enterprises without Melvin was not all it was cracked up to be, and it had taken a toll on the once-attractive Shirley Reine. She had let herself go. Her short skirts were gone, replaced by stretchy jogging suits. Her hair had been cropped shorter than Wanda Reine's had been when she vanished. She didn't bother putting in her contact lenses and wore eyeglasses every day. She didn't wear any makeup, not even lipstick. Shirley's good looks had been drained with her nonstop schedule, just as her energy had been drained by her husband's antics years earlier. She was only 49 but she felt like she was 89.

So when she saw the police cruisers pull into the Reine compound just before 10 a.m. on August 29, 2002, with lights and sirens blazing just so everyone in Falmouth could know the law was on the clan's corner—again—Shirley just smiled to herself. It figured. She also smiled at Falmouth Police Chief David Cusolito when he handed her the search warrant he had obtained to search her house at 657 East Falmouth Highway and the offices of Five Star Enterprises. "We are looking to recover a number of items alleged to have been stolen."

She welcomed the cops inside and offered to put on a pot of coffee. She knew they would be there for a while, and she could use a cup herself. She listened as drawers were opened and closed and as furniture was pulled away from walls in her home. Pictures were pulled off walls as cops looked for hidden safes. Clothes were strewn on the floors of closets as they were ransacked. There were cops on their hands and knees searching under rugs. Others leafed through the pages of picture books. Outside the house, state police went to work in the yard where the trucks were stored for Five Star Enterprises. Other cops involved in the raid went to the office above her garage and started to rifle through Five Star Enterprises paperwork, bills and books.

Right after 3 p.m., Cusolito came into the kitchen to announce that Shirley Reine was going to be arrested and charged with possession of a gun and stolen property. She did not cry. She did not plead. She simply thrust out her small wrists and waited for the click of the cuffs.

"Mrs. Reine. You are under arrest for possession of an unlicensed firearm, unlicensed possession of ammunition, and receiving a stolen motor vehicle," Cusolito recited to Shirley Reine. Then he asked her to put her wrists behind her back and pushed the handcuffs tight. He took her by the elbow, escorted her out to a cruiser, put a strong hand on her head and guided her into the back seat. It was devastating for her. Her picture was splashed on the front pages of the local papers. The headline on the *Cape Cod Times* story read: "Police Arrest Falmouth Trash Hauler." The story began:

After an extensive search of several buildings at two properties owned by Five Star Enterprises, police

arrested one of the owners of the Falmouth trash hauling business, which has been the subject of recent
charges of environmental violations. Shirley M. Reine,
49, of 657 East Falmouth Highway, was charged with
possession of an unlicensed firearm, a .357 Magnum
revolver, unlicensed possession of ammunition; and
receiving a stolen motor vehicle. A 1977 Ford four-
wheel-drive pickup truck reported stolen from Westport was recovered at the East Falmouth Road
property. Reine was released last evening.

Police had found everything just where Todd Reine told
them it would be. Shirley had a gun secreted in a diaper bag
hidden in her bedroom closet. The .357 Magnum had also
been reported stolen, investigators would later discover.
There was a stolen 1977 Ford four-wheel-drive pickup truck
that had been reported ripped off from the Massachusetts
town of Westport years earlier. There was also a backhoe on
the property that Shirley could not provide the proper paperwork for.

What police did not expect to find, however, was a box of
lascivious videotapes that featured Shirley Reine in various sex
acts with recognizable men of Falmouth. One of the men was
Michael Domingues, her employee and friend. Domingues
would later claim that he was one of Melvin Reine's many
illegitimate children, and therefore would not have had an
affair with his stepmother. But investigators disputed his
rationale, especially after they viewed the tapes. Michael
Domingues was reputedly on them. Domingues continues to
deny that. In interviews, he denies the existence of a sex tape
with Shirley, and says his relationship with Shirley was appropriate. There were other powerful men from Falmouth on
them too. The tapes have since been locked away by Cape and
Islands District Attorney Michael O'Keefe. Rumors have
abounded since about exactly who'd had sex with Shirley
Reine. It was unclear why Shirley had videotaped the sexual
encounters, but cops knew that there were men on those tapes

from Falmouth who would do almost anything to make sure that the existence of the videos was never revealed.

Just months before Shirley's arrest, Falmouth officials had filed a civil action lawsuit against her for the dump that Melvin had left behind when he was committed. After Shirley Reine was transported to the Falmouth police station so her arrest could be processed, police moved the search to the Old Barnstable Road dumping ground where a search was conducted until roughly 5 p.m.—ostensibly for stolen cars, but investigators had hoped to stumble upon the remains of people close to Melvin who had disappeared. State police cadaver dogs combed the area, sniffing under the demolition debris and abandoned cars. Investigators thought the search could bring peace of mind to the families of Wanda Reine or Paul Alwardt. At least a proper burial for Wanda. It was not to be. The cadaver dogs never found a thing.

At the Falmouth police station, Shirley used her one phone call to dial her husband's criminal attorney, Frederick Mycock. The lawyer pointed out that Shirley had no prior criminal history and she was released on personal recognizance hours after her arrest. Mycock issued a statement to reporters who had been digging into Melvin Reine's criminal history since his commitment, saying:

"You will find this arrest is the result of a family feud between Mrs. Reine and the sons of her husband who have discovered they have been disinherited. Police found a gun but obviously my client knew nothing about that."

Mycock did not talk about the sex tapes. It is not a crime to cheat on your husband. Nor is it a crime to want to review that adultery on a videotape later. He did, however, talk about the Reine boys. It was no secret that Todd and Melvin Reine Jr. had led police to Shirley Reine's house. Todd said as much.

"Yeah, I talked to the cops," he blurted on that day he met a writer in the parking lot of a Plymouth eatery. "I wanted to put pressure on her so they could find out what happened to my mother. They'll make it sound evil that we talked about Shirley to the police, but that's why we did it.

We talked to the police in June, they didn't go in until August. What took so long?"

Mycock saw the situation differently. Wasn't it possible that the boys had planted the gun there to set Shirley up? It was clear that there was no love lost between the Reine boys and their stepmother. That feud that Mycock had referred to in his statement to reporters was all in black and white, part of the ongoing civil court proceedings that was playing out in Barnstable Superior Court. *Reine v. Reine* was an ugly case indeed. Most family feuds are.

But things were about to get a lot uglier.

SEVENTEEN

Melvin Reine Jr. and Todd Reine did not mince words when they filed suit against their stepmother. She was a conniving thief who took advantage of their father's deteriorating mental state and used "undue influence" over him to get him to transfer ownership of his assets to her. The boys were claiming that the paperwork their father had signed was fraudulent. Their lawyers listed a litany of complaints against Shirley trying to prove their claim:

1. On or before late 1999, while he had behaved strangely on some occasions before, it was very clear to his son Todd Reine that his father was having serious mental troubles.

2. By late 2000 his deteriorating mental condition really started to manifest itself. Melvin Sr. went to pick up a container behind Kenyon Market where there was a moving truck blocking the container. When a woman came out and said she would have it moved, he went into a rage and started to lift the moving truck up with the forks of the truck he was driving. The woman pleaded with him to stop and at this time he told her he would blow her head off with a shotgun. The police were called and when they arrived, they arrested him.

3. Over the next several months during 2001, leading up to Melvin Sr.'s commitment to Taunton State Hospital, his

odd behavior continued and was becoming more frequent.

4. During the summer of 2001, Todd would visit his children at their home near his father's and Melvin Sr. would see Todd there and come over on several occasions. They would talk, but Melvin Sr. clearly could not have a meaningful conversation. In the middle of talking about something specific, he would jump to another topic completely different. That happened frequently and he would constantly repeat himself over and over.

5. Others who have known Melvin have concluded that he was irrational and mentally ill based on his speech and behavior throughout 2001.

6. In one conversation between Melvin and Roman Medeiros, Captain of the Falmouth Police and Melvin's former brother-in-law, Melvin Sr. behaved erratically. He was rambling on and on and on and not able to maintain a clear train of thought. His subject matter jumped from one topic to another and back again. It was clear to Mr. Medeiros that he was having mental health issues.

7. After Mr. Medeiros' conversation with Melvin, he had several interactions with the police department and citizens of the community exhibiting bizarre and unusual behavior which led up to his being criminally charged and committed to a mental health facility.

8. Late summer of 2001, a longtime friend and employee of Melvin Sr., Sonny "Caesar" Pena told Melvin Jr. that he noticed his father had been acting differently lately. Caesar told Melvin Jr. that while having dinner at The Boathouse Restaurant in Falmouth, Melvin Sr. could not carry on a conversation, was fidgety, kept looking all around and would repeat things over and over.

9. In spring of 2001, Melvin Sr. pulled Melvin Jr. over on Old Barnstable Road, Falmouth, while he was working on a residential trash pickup route. Melvin Sr. was rambling on about getting Melvin Jr. to come see the garage and he would not get out of the truck until Melvin Jr. agreed to look at the garage. When they got to the garage, Melvin Sr. was rambling incoherently.

10. Susana Augusta is a friend of Melvin Jr. She told him that in the spring of 2001, Melvin Sr. was driving down Route 28 in Waquoit. He stopped the truck in the middle of the road and got out of the truck and was walking aimlessly around the truck. He got back in the truck and proceeded about ½ mile and got out of the truck again and on foot circled the truck numerous times. He got back in the truck again and drove until he reached the top of the hill approximately 10 yards from the entrance of Five Star. Again, he got out of his truck and approached Susan Augusta, who was in the car driving behind him.

11. He insisted that Susan, who had never met Melvin Sr. before, pull into his driveway because he needed to show her something. After saying no several times, Susan finally relented and maneuvered her car onto Melvin Sr.'s property. At this time, he led her to the lower garage of the property where a BMW was being stored. He told her it was his BMW (which it wasn't) and that she needed to leave her car at this site so he could clean and wax her car. She explained that she had to go to work. He told her to drop it off that coming Sunday and he will clean and wax it at that time. She said "okay" so she could leave as soon as possible.

12. Based on many conversations, most of Melvin Sr.'s family, including his brothers and sisters, have known for years that Melvin Sr. has been mentally unbalanced, easily confused and disoriented and has engaged in

erratic and bizarre behavior, especially since the year 2000.

13. On August 2, 2001, the day that Melvin Sr. signed the agreement turning over the ownership of Five Star to Shirley for no consideration, according to Shirley, he was disabled with Alzheimer's.

14. Thereafter Melvin Reine signed a general power of attorney in favor of Shirley.

15. In July 2001, Shirley took title to four parcels of real estate, as trustee, which Melvin Sr. had transferred into an irrevocable trust of which Todd and Melvin Jr. were the sole beneficiaries.

16. This transfer violated the terms of the trust.

17. Melvin Sr. was found mentally incompetent to stand trial on criminal charges filed against him on October 9, 2001, and subsequently was committed to Taunton State Hospital.

18. Todd, Melvin Reine Jr. and Melvin Sr. all worked for Five Star at one time and cooperatively sold part of the business, in two steps. The first step was to settle a lawsuit with the Town of Falmouth to pay outstanding bills and the second was to provide for Melvin Sr.'s retirement.

19. All three signed a non-compete agreement for five years and the plan was that Todd and Melvin Jr. would work for the buyer of the company while Melvin Sr. would run the remaining portion of the business, which was small enough for one person to handle.

20. They had agreed that Melvin Sr. would not sell off any assets, which he did not, and after five years Todd and

Melvin Jr. would resume running the sanitation business. At that time, the company would be Melvin Jr.'s and Todd's and Melvin Sr. would draw a salary for part-time driving and advisory role.

21. Shirley has been selling off assets belonging to Todd as well as assets belonging to Melvin Jr.

22. Shirley continues to have control over other valuable assets and family heirlooms, such as cars and farm implements that Melvin Sr. has told Todd that he wants his children and grandchildren to have.

23. Shirley has pending criminal charges, including larceny of motor vehicles, receiving stolen property and other offenses in connection with the assets of Five Star.

24. Shirley has also already been caught violating the preliminary injunction, admittedly selling for $42,000 a trailer used in Five Star's business after being served with the preliminary injunction explicitly prohibiting such sales.

The list of grievances against Shirley Reine continued in the lawsuit. Todd and Melvin Jr.'s lawyers took affidavits from everyone who knew the elder Reine: his brother John, his neighbors, his friends.

But the strangest deposition filed in the case came from Roman "Skip" Medeiros, the Falmouth police detective captain. Wanda's brother. Most of the cops on the Falmouth force thought it odd that Medeiros maintained a friendly relationship with Melvin Sr. even after his sister had vanished and was presumed murdered by her husband. Medeiros did not care what people thought. The boys were his nephews. In order to have a relationship with them, he had to be nice to Melvin Reine. The affidavit he gave on behalf of his nephews was telling:

1. I have been a police officer in the town of Falmouth since June of 1975 and was promoted to detective captain in May of 1999.

2. In the spring of 1999, the defendant Shirley Reine called me at the police department stating that her husband Melvin would like to meet with me in front of the police station. Shortly after that, Melvin arrived.

3. I had spoken to Melvin over the years. Melvin is my former brother-in-law, having been married to my sister Wanda, who mysteriously disappeared in 1971.

4. The conversation with Melvin was erratic and all over the place. He was rambling on and on and not able to maintain a clear train of thought. His subject matter jumped from one topic to another and back again. It was clear to me that he was having mental health issues.

5. I have known Melvin most of my life. Melvin taught me how to drive a truck and bought me my first gun. I spent a considerable amount of time with Melvin in earlier years. There was no doubt throughout this conversation that Melvin wasn't acting rationally.

6. After my meeting with Melvin he had several interactions with the police department and citizens of the community with bizarre and unusual behavior which led up to his being criminally charged and committed to a mental health facility.

Nowhere in his affidavit did Medeiros mention that Melvin Reine had rear-ended his police cruiser decades earlier in an unprovoked attack. He also did not mention that Melvin Reine had escaped any criminal prosecution in that case and was merely forced to write the town of Falmouth a check for $356 to cover the damage to the cruiser. Nor did Medeiros say whether he harbored any resentment against Melvin Reine for his sister's unexplained disappearance. It remained unclear what Medeiros had to gain by getting involved with an ugly lawsuit his nephews filed against their de facto mother, which would be how Shirley would describe herself in court records where her lawyers argued that she was entitled to the family business. When asked about the case, Medeiros refused to talk. Over and over again.

Shirley's attorneys countered that Melvin Sr. was rational on that summer day in 2001 when he walked into the office of his civil attorney James H. Smith and told him he wanted to transfer his stocks in the company to Shirley. Smith gave an affidavit in the case that read:

Melvin and I discussed the matter and he informed me that he had not been feeling that well of late and was not able to participate fully with the operation of Five Star Enterprises. He further told me that Shirley Reine had effectively been operating the business for a while and he wanted her to have the business because she had been running it for some time. She was his wife and he did not wish for his sons, Melvin J. Reine Jr. and Todd Reine to have any part of the business or its assets.

I explained to Melvin that upon execution of the stock transfer document that he would no longer own any part of the business or its assets and Shirley would own all of them.

Melvin stated that he understood that by transferring his shares of stock to Shirley, he would no longer own any of the business or its assets, that he would no longer own an interest in the business. That was fine with him and he wanted Shirley to have the business.

At the time the document transferring his shares of stock to Shirley Reine was executed, there was nothing about Melvin J. Reine Sr.'s appearance, demeanor, conversation or responsiveness to questions that caused me to have any concerns about his competency to execute this document:

On or about October 18, 2001 Melvin J. Reine Sr. came to my office to execute a durable power of attorney; at this time I was aware that Melvin had allegedly engaged in criminal activity.

Because of this allegation of criminal activity, I took extra caution in talking to Melvin and explaining the nature of the document he was about to execute in order to ensure that he knew what he was signing and that his execution of the document was his free act and deed.

Melvin stated that he understood what he was doing, he was concerned that there were times in the recent past when he had acted somewhat irrationally and in the event he was no longer capable of handling his own affairs or taking care of himself, he wanted Shirley to handle his affairs and take care of him.

The attorney signed and dated the document and it became part of Shirley Reine's argument that her husband's relationship with the boys had deteriorated much faster than his mental state. She was just carrying out his will—even if it would cost her everything. She presented her own case in court with the help of her attorney William Enright.

The defendant, Shirley M. Reine, married Melvin Sr. Reine on October 20, 1999. The two had cohabitated together since 1972. Melvin Sr. Reine is the father of the plaintiffs, Todd M. Reine and Melvin Reine Jr. Shirley Reine is not the defendants' mother.

On August 2, 2001, Melvin Reine Sr. transferred his interest in Five Star Enterprises to his wife Shirley. Shirley had been running the business for some time prior to August 2, 2001 while the plaintiffs had no involvement whatsoever in the business. In or about the year 2000, Five Star Enterprises was the subject of much negative publicity relative to the discovery of allegedly improperly disposed of construction materials. In or about January 2003, Shirley M. Reine conveyed the assets of Five Star Enterprises to pay off a debt to the town of Falmouth.

Shirley Reine gave her own affidavit in the case. The tone of her deposition was telling. She was depressed about the way the case was being handled. She could not have a relationship with the men she had helped raise, or their children, whom she considered grandkids. She was getting old and the only person she had in her corner was her sister Loretta Gilfoy and Loretta's son, her nephew. She was having dinner with Loretta every night by now just to quell the incessant loneliness she felt every time she drove into her house on the Reine compound and walked into a house filled with no people, just her dogs, her babies. All of that was clear in her deposition.

I helped raised the plaintiffs and was their de-facto mother since they were about the ages of 5 and 6.

I had been running Five Star Enterprises for some period of time prior to this conveyance of the business to me. Neither of the plaintiffs were involved in the operation of Five Star Enterprises. In or about the summer of 2000, Five Star Enterprises made headlines for alleged improper disposal of construction debris.

In late November 2001, my husband was committed to Taunton State Hospital. As the result of attending to my husband's medical needs and the negative publicity attendant to the allegation of improper disposal of construction debris, the business of Five Star Enterprises declined.

Additionally, I had to expend approximately $28,000 to pay for the cleanup of the allegedly improperly disposed of construction materials.

Thus from the summer of 2000 to the early winter of 2002, Five Star Enterprises operated at a loss and had to sell certain assets in order to generate sufficient cash to pay for the afore-mentioned cleanup, keep other obligations up to date and keep the business operating.

In an effort to regenerate the business of disposing of construction debris, I determined to form a new corporation and transfer the assets of Five Star Enterprises Inc., hopeful that prospective customers would not make the association between Five Star Enterprises and the new corporation.

In January, 2003, S&M/Five Star Demolition was formed and it continues to conduct removing and disposing of construction debris.

She signed the document on September 24, 2003. In less than two years, she would be dead. She would be shot at point-blank range upon returning from dinner with her sister Loretta and her nephew. Nothing was stolen from her wallet. Her alleged lover had an alibi that he provided to investigators and would prove to be incredibly cooperative in the investigation.

Investigators continue to believe that the land and the assets at the center of the *Reine v. Reine* dispute, the property that Shirley Reine was trying to protect, provided the motive for her murder.

EIGHTEEN

William Enright had never remembered seeing his client look so rattled. Enright was a compactly built man, yet still hard. His years in the military had given him a no-nonsense exterior. He was not a man to be messed with, which is one of the reasons that Shirley Reine had grown to trust and respect him. Enright had watched Shirley Reine's demeanor and appearance begin its slow deterioration years earlier, but he still could not help but notice that she had taken on that distant look of someone who was compelled to remind herself to breathe. She held her breath for long stretches of time, then sucked in a deep one when her lungs protested. It was clear that anxiety attacks consumed her and that the panic left her gasping for air.

She had every reason to suffer anxiety attacks. After her arrest, her husband had heard that she had been promiscuous and somehow, he was coherent enough to confront her on it. She was embroiled in an ugly lawsuit with her stepsons and had to confront them at the Reine compound constantly. Shirley had taken to eating dinner with her sister Loretta Gilfoy and her nephew every night just to avoid the tension. She was clearly worried, and Enright was trying to help her navigate the *Reine v. Reine* lawsuit, her problems with the federal environmental types who wanted fines for the illegal dump and the demands from the town of Falmouth, also angry about the mess at Old Barnstable Road.

"Shirley had business acumen," Enright explained. "She was trying to consolidate parts of the business in order to pay off debt and keep Five Star alive. She was doing the right thing, but those boys couldn't see past what they wanted. The boys' lawsuit was bankrupting the business."

Enright remembered that two weeks before his client would be found dead, he accompanied Shirley and her friend Michael Domingues to a tour of the Old Barnstable Road dumping ground. That day will now haunt him for the rest of his life. It was a walkthrough of the property orchestrated by Todd and Melvin Jr.'s attorneys. They wanted to make sure that Shirley Reine was really spending business assets taking care of the cleanup, as she claimed in court records. In one filing, Todd pointed out that:

> "by illegally disposing of huge quantities of construction debris and other solid waste, the defendants Melvin, Shirley and Five Star have unreasonably interfered with the use and enjoyment of the property on Barnstable Road owned by the plaintiffs. The defendants are liable to the plaintiffs for the costs of removing and abating the effects of the illegal debris and diminution in the value of their interest in the property on Barnstable Road."

Not only did Todd want the parcel of land—he wanted it only after Shirley Reine footed the bill cleaning it up.

The boys studied every detail of the cleanup process with their lawyers. No one spoke as they moved over the property. Todd Reine carried a digital camera and took shots of everything on it: the three-bay garage and the heavy equipment inside of it, the acreage that had been cleared of construction debris, even photographs of William Enright and Shirley. The lawyer saw that as an intimidation tactic, but he did not confront Todd. Neither did Shirley. Of the two boys, Todd was considered the most like his father. He had a temper and a vicious streak and it was better not to poke him with a verbal stick. Enright and Shirley were walking "15 to 20 feet" ahead of Todd Reine when they heard him make a declaration, speaking, Enright recalled, in "a very loud voice" that was clearly meant to be overheard: "This case will never go to trial."

Shirley turned to him and began to whisper. "He's right. The boys are going to see that this case does not go to trial."

Enright tried to calm her down. "Relax, Shirley. That is not going to happen."

Shirley's fears would not be assuaged. She was on the verge of tears and had started to breathe heavily enough that Enright noticed the shift. "If anything happens to me, tell the world it was Todd and Melvin. Make me that promise. Tell everyone it was Todd and Melvin."

Enright was a civil attorney. He was a longtime military man who held the rank of colonel in the Air National Guard. While he was small in stature, he still had the presence of a man who was used to giving orders. Compactly built, he still commanded respect and was not used to anyone having the gall to question his authority. Despite all that, Todd and Melvin made him nervous. He regretted taking on Shirley Reine as a client and wished he had never become embroiled in this ugly fight between a woman married to a madman and that whacko's sons. He was aware that Todd and Melvin Reine were the architects of the 2003 raid on Shirley's house, a case that he referred to as "a crock of shit." A judge agreed—only he used different terms—and he chastised the police for using information garnered by defendants embroiled in a lawsuit with Shirley Reine as the basis for the search warrant, and dismissed all charges against her. It did not change the fact that everyone in law enforcement was now aware that the Falmouth Fox's wife had strange sexual habits, and shared that information with men in the town. Enright rarely dealt with criminals, and underestimated what Shirley Reine was saying to him. He would later wish that he had taken her more seriously.

"I knew Todd was obsessed. In his mind it was his business. The boys and their father had been estranged for a number of years, but in Todd's mind, the trash company was rightfully his. The ugliest lawsuits out there are families fighting over money," he would say. "I know that the boys don't like me. And I know that Shirley was right to be afraid of her stepsons. The saddest thing about the case is that Shirley was truly devoted to their father. She really loved Melvin. He was the true love of her life. She would always talk about how often she visited Melvin and how she wanted to bring a touch of love to his life every day."

Enright had no qualms about pointing the finger at Todd and Melvin on May 10, 2005. He had not even sipped his morning cup of coffee when he got a panicked phone call from Michael Domingues. The man was hysterical and screaming into the phone:

"Bill, Shirley's dead! She's murdered."

Enright—like Domingues—had one thought as he grappled with the idea that his client had been assassinated: *Todd and Melvin did this.* It was a theory that he was all too willing to share with anyone who asked, as Shirley had requested that day they walked through the Old Barnstable Road dump.

"I truly believe those boys had something to do with Shirley Reine's death."

Enright was not the only one who thought that way.

NINETEEN

It was five days before Christmas in 2002 and Shirley Reine had a lot to do. She wanted to pick up a few nice shirts to drop off at the hospital for Melvin. She wanted to buy a gift for Michael Domingues, her coworker and intimate friend. As she pulled into her garage just after 8 p.m. that night she sucked in a deep breath and tried to enjoy her surroundings. The anxiety that had plagued her for months since the boys filed their lawsuit had dissipated slightly with the mood of the season. Christmas lights twinkled off the houses lining Route 28; the snow over the cranberry bog pond was picturesque. For that brief minute, all was okay in Shirley Reine's world.

Then she noticed that her dogs were running around the inside of the garage. Shirley Reine had never had children of her own and got a lot of comfort from her dogs. She called them her "babies." She did a head count of the dogs and noticed one was missing.

It was a bracingly cold night, and she had no idea how six of the seven dogs had managed to get loose from inside the house. She called out to the missing dachshund, but did not hear the scratching of his paws on the concrete floor. He must have gotten outside.

All of that peace she had felt just minutes before was completely gone. Her dog was outside in the cold. But worse, someone had to have been in the house to let the dogs into the garage, and to let one outside in the cold.

She picked up her cell phone and called her sister Loretta.

"Loretta, have you been to the house?" Even as she said it, she knew it was a stupid question. She had just left her sister, and there was no way Loretta could have beaten her to East Falmouth Highway, let herself into the house and then left before Shirley got home.

"No, why would I have been there?" Loretta responded.

"The dogs are loose."

Loretta felt a chill. She knew that wasn't right. Someone had to have gotten inside. In her confusion, she gave her sister bad advice. She should have said, "Run!" or even "Call the police." Instead she said:

"Why don't you go inside and check the house and see if anything is wrong?"

Shirley noted that the door was secured, locked even. But there were pry marks on the exterior of the door and the doorframe. The door that led from the garage into the interior of the house was slightly ajar. She walked inside and found that the two dog gates she used to keep her babies from running through the house had been moved. She immediately raced to the bedroom and found that her drawers and her jewelry cabinet had been rifled through.

More alarming, the two-foot-square, light beige safe she had secreted in a closet was gone. Whoever had taken it was not after money or jewels—they were after the slew of important papers, including Melvin Reine's will and her will that she had stashed inside. She began to cry. There was no question in her mind who'd stolen her paperwork. Todd Reine had been asking for a copy of his father's will, and she'd refused to give him one.

As she emerged from the house, she saw her sister outside talking to the mother of Todd Reine's children, who was trying to help search for the missing dog. Loretta saw the distressed look on her sister's face and wordlessly called 911.

A Falmouth police cruiser was dispatched to the scene but so was State Police Trooper Kimberly Squier of the Cape and Islands Detective Unit. The state police recognized the address because of the ongoing investigation int

Melvin and Shirley Reine and the Five Star Enterprises illegal dumping ground. The state police were handling that matter, and it made sense to have a trooper present now that there was a theft reported from the Reine compound.

"There were important papers in there," Shirley told the trooper. "Papers the boys want. My husband's will, my will, other documents. It was my stepsons. They are upset that their father wrote them out of the will, and they are taking me to court. They want to destroy the will or change it."

The crime-scene unit tried to lift prints from the bedroom. There were none. Whoever had taken the safe had covered their hands. It was clearly not the work of harried teens looking for some gold chains or diamond rings they could sell off. Todd Reine was questioned, but he had an alibi. Reports were written, but there was nothing the Falmouth cops or the state police could do that night.

Strangely enough, months later, on January 11, 2003, Falmouth cop Kent Clarkson got a call from his boss, Detective Captain Roman Medeiros. The commander started to talk about a stash of papers that his nephew Todd Reine had received from "an unidentified black male" who had apparently stopped by Todd Reine's house just out of the kindness of his heart. The "unidentified black male" did not demand any monetary reward or say why he'd decided to hand over the neat pile to Todd when it belonged to Shirley. The documents included a trust agreement involving Shirley and Melvin Reine, miscellaneous paperwork involving Five Star Enterprises and current wills for Melvin Sr. and Shirley Reine. Of course, Medeiros said that Todd had no idea who the mysterious black man was or how he'd known Todd might be looking for those very documents to help in the civil case he had filed against his stepmother.

Clarkson did not hold the rank to grill the veteran police captain, so he simply walked into Medeiros' office and took the pile of papers. He made copies of everything for his own files and then called Shirley Reine's attorney, who was still listed on her intake sheet from the night she'd been arrested and charged with possession of an unregistered handgun and bullets, and receiving stolen property. "Mr. Mycock," the cop said when the attorney picked up the phone, "I think we have recovered some stolen property that belongs to your client." Fred Mycock called Shirley's civil attorney Bill Enright and they picked up the papers to return them to Shirley.

With that, the paperwork was returned and the burglary was largely forgotten by investigators. That is, until Shirley Reine was murdered.

Only then did a local thug named Jerome Bradley make a phone call to the state police. He was nervous. He had information, he said, regarding a home invasion at Shirley Reine's house and he wanted to spill his guts as long as investigators did not try to pin her murder on him. State Trooper Kimberly Squier went to meet with Bradley.

He demanded a deal that would give him immunity. Because there were very few leads in the Reine case, the district attorney gave Squier the green light to hammer out a cooperation agreement. Then Bradley began to talk, starting his story with details about a phone call he'd received from his friend John Rams, a recently released convicted killer, on a December night in 2002.

"We have to do a favor for Uncle Todd," Rams said. "Come over."

Bradley's girlfriend dropped him off at Rams' home on Wareham Lake Shore Drive.

Rams was an intimidating guy. In 1992 he'd gotten into a brawl at the Onset Bandshell on Cape Cod with a 23-year-old man and stabbed him a dozen times. The victim died a short time later, and Rams would be convicted of manslaughter. He only served 7 years in prison for that crime, and he did not clean up his act when he got out.

"Who's Uncle Todd?" Bradley asked.

"You know, Reine. The Falmouth Fox's kid. Todd Reine," Rams said. "We gotta get a safe in his stepmother's bedroom. There's something in it for us. There is ten thousand dollars in cash. All he wants is the safe."

Bradley was on board. "Okay then. We need to find a crowbar, a tire iron."

The two men went outside and began to ransack a work shed that belonged to Rams' father. They found a foot-long screwdriver and took a tire iron out of Rams' car. Rams picked up his Nextel phone and called Todd Reine.

"We're on our way to do that now," Rams reported.

Rams was dating a woman named Nadia Smuliac. She was a woman attracted to bad boys, and Rams certainly fit the bill.

"Come on, baby," Rams told her. "We are taking a ride."

The three of them climbed into her Grand Prix. Nadia was behind the wheel. John Rams sat beside her and Jerome Bradley sat in the back seat. No one spoke as they made their way to Falmouth. When they got to the Reine compound, they drove past the circle of homes a number of times, noting the rock with the Reine etching in front. Nadia navigated the car to an area behind the Five Star Enterprises garages. Rams and Bradley pulled on leather gloves and began to walk to Shirley Reine's garage door. Bradley peeked in the windows and heard the dogs barking. There was no car in the garage and it appeared that Shirley was not home. He jumped from foot to foot, nervous. There were a lot of houses in the Reine compound and at any time someone could look out the window.

"Let's just do this," Bradley said. "Someone's gonna see us."

Bradley jimmied the screwdriver into the doorframe of the garage. After a bit of prying, the door loosened. He grabbed the tire iron, and the door popped open. The two of them went inside. The dogs barking in the dark garage freaked out the burglars. Bradley went back outside thinking that Shirley Reine was in fact home.

"I'm going to smash that bitch in the fucking head," Rams said. He made his way into the house and emerged a few minutes later. "There ain't nobody here."

Rams opened the garage door leading into the house, and the dogs launched onto his ankles. He began to kick them out of the way as Bradley followed behind him. They walked through the kitchen, passed the living room and climbed up a flight of stairs leading to Shirley Reine's bedroom. Todd Reine knew the house well. He'd grown up there. He had given Rams careful instructions on where his stepmother's bedroom was and where they could find the safe.

At first, Bradley found a small lockbox and tossed it to Rams.

"I can smell all this, all the jewelry, all the fucking jewelry," Rams said.

"Leave it. We're only here for one thing. We're here for the safe and for the $10,000 prize. That's it. We need to get Todd his present."

Rams took the lockbox and tucked it inside his jacket. He pulled the zipper tight so the jacket would hold the lockbox secure, and the two men went to work.

Bradley picked up the safe and started to carry it down the stairs. Halfway down he began to hyperventilate. "This fucking thing is heavy. Where the fuck are you?"

Rams had already made his way through the kitchen and was entering the garage. He turned around and snarled.

"Shut the fuck up. You want the whole neighborhood to hear you? Jesus Christ!"

Bradley carried the safe toward Nadia's car. Halfway there, he tripped over a wooden border to Shirley's garden, and fell. The safe flew to the ground with a thud, even in the cushion of snow. At this point, Rams was nowhere to be found. They had established before going in that Rams would meet up with Nadia, and the two of them would return to pick up Bradley and the safe. After a few minutes, Bradley began to get nervous when the Grand Prix did not pull down Route 28 to pick him up. He returned to the area behind the garage and began to pace back and forth. He sat on a ledge and waited. After what seemed like hours in the freezing cold, he saw headlights pull in behind the garage.

"What the fuck? Where were you?" Bradley screeched.

Rams wordlessly picked up the safe and put it in the trunk. Then he turned his attention to Bradley.

"You didn't follow the plan. I told you to go to the parking lot where the deli and liquor store was."

The ride back to Wareham was tense. But they still had a job to do. Once they arrived back at Rams' house they lugged the safe down to the private beach about forty feet down a hill.

"How the fuck we gonna open this?" Bradley asked.

"Let's do it caveman-style," Rams said.

They went back into the shed and pulled out a sledge-hammer and began to pound away at the safe. After about five straight minutes of beatings the door popped open. Bradley looked in and became infuriated.

"There is no fucking money in here. Not a dime."

Rams was elated. "Yeah, but Uncle Todd's present is in here."

He fanned out the paperwork in the safe as if it were a fist-ful of hundreds he'd just scooped up off a blackjack table.

"This right here is worth millions to Todd. It's his fa-ther's last will and testament."

Rams grabbed his Nextel again.

"Hey, Uncle, we got the prize."

Just over a half-hour later, Todd Reine arrived at Rams' house. Rams handed him the paperwork.

"There was no money in there, guy," Bradley said to Todd.

Todd simply said, "Don't worry about it," and climbed back into his car. Bradley was steamed. Rams tried to calm him down.

"Uncle Todd will take care of you, I'm tellin' ya. Let's get rid of this thing."

The two men then heaved the safe into the water at the end of the beach area, wading in about ten feet from the sandy shoreline. That spring, the Wareham Beach Associa-tion held its annual cleanup of the waterfront at Agawam Lake Shores. In 2003 they found a safe in the water right next to John Rams' home.

All of this was recounted to Trooper Squier, who inter-viewed and recorded Jerome Bradley. Another Trooper, Tim Finn, was also present at the interview. The date was June 2, 2005. Shirley Reine had been dead for just over two weeks.

After Bradley described the burglary, Squier began to ask him about Todd's relationship to Shirley Reine.

"Did you ever hear Todd talk about his stepmother?"

"Occasionally. Just nasty, disgusting stuff about how he despised and hated her. 'Wish she was dead,' if I remember correctly. I didn't hear him say, 'I'm going to have her killed,' but 'I wish that fuckin' bitch was dead.' Other than that, I didn't really— You know what I mean? He was just very— You know, not much of a talker."

Squier then asked about John Rams. Did he ever talk about Shirley Reine?

"I heard John, you know, he said, 'I'll take care of that fuckin' bitch.' He's like, 'I'll get rid of her.' I remember hearing that a few times. You know . . . I believe that he— You know what I mean, he— I believe he did that. He did say he was going to kill her and blah, blah, blah. But I've heard him say he was going to kill a lot of people too. But the thing— The fact of the matter is that he is a killer and he has killed before."

Bradley then told investigators he did not talk to Rams for about a month after the robbery. A few months later, Rams was back in prison anyhow after he beat up Nadia, in violation of his parole. He tried to make it up to her by presenting her with a gift he'd pulled out of the lockbox at the robbery scene: a Cartier diamond ring. All was forgiven, briefly.

Then Nadia heard about the grand jury that had been convened to hear evidence against her boyfriend. At least one man testified that he'd heard Rams shoot off his mouth at a party about how the ring he'd given Nadia was connected to the "Shirley Reine murder." After that, she'd driven to the Falmouth Police Department to turn the ring over to police herself. She didn't have to worry about Rams coming after her for cooperating with investigators. He had been arrested again, this time testing positive for drugs.

As the grand jury heard from witnesses, state police troopers assigned to the Shirley Reine investigation took a ride to MCI–Norfolk, the Massachusetts prison where John Rams was being held. Trooper Chris Mason told Rams they were there to "speak to him about an incident regarding Todd Reine."

Rams responded by blasting Mason for being unsympathetic to his plight during the last interview he'd sat for. In that one, Rams told police that Todd Reine had offered to buy him a video store in Wareham if he were to kill Shirley. He used this visit from the cops to reiterate that story, rambling about his plans to take a video store from Todd Reine and eventually convert it into a pornography and head shop. The problem with Rams' story was that he had little credibility. He had been a snitch for a long time, and some of his grandiose stories were eventually revealed as total falsehoods. Rams' claims were not enough—yet—to link Todd Reine to Shirley's murder. Of course, Rams also told the investigators that he'd had no plans to actually kill Shirley for the video store, but he'd wanted to hear out Todd Reine on the plan.

Mason wrote it up on his report, dated September 20, 2006, this way:

Rams was brought to a conference room located on the second floor of the administrative building at MCI–Norfolk. I then advised Rams that I wished to speak with him about an incident regarding Todd Reine. Rams then spent several minutes telling me that he felt I had been unsympathetic to his plight the last time I had interviewed him. Rams stated that I was lucky he didn't tell me to "go fuck yourself" and that although his lawyer had told him not to speak, he was going to speak to me anyway.

I informed Rams that I was aware that he had an attorney for his probation violation and the grand jury investigating Shirley Reine's homicide, but that I wanted to speak to him about a different crime which directly affected him. Rams again stated that he had nothing to be concerned about and that he was willing to tell me everything about Reine despite his attorney's advice.

(Rams had motive to rat out Reine. After he was locked up, Todd Reine had taken up with Nadia.)

I then asked Rams if I could record the interview and Miranda rights by means of a digital recorder. Rams stated that he would not speak on a recorder. I then asked Rams if he would be willing to execute an electronic recording refusal form, which he did at approximately 9:10 hours. Rams checked all of the boxes indicating "No." I then read Rams his Miranda rights from a printed form and provided him with a copy of the same. At approximately 9:15 a.m. hours Rams executed a waiver of his Miranda rights.

Rams then launched into an unsolicited review of information he had previously given me, outlining a meeting he claimed to have had with police in which he told police that Reine had asked him to kill his step-mother Shirley Reine.

I told Rams I was interested in a different situation with Todd Reine. I asked Rams what he could tell me about a breaking and entering which had occurred at Shirley Reine's house. Rams remained silent. I informed Rams that a grand jury had received information about that incident and that a safe was alleged to have been taken and that Rams was said to have been involved and to have done the break for Todd Reine. Rams was then asked what if anything he was to get in payment for the job. Rams stated that Todd Reine was going to give him something for killing Shirley Reine and that Reine had offered to buy him a video store for killing Shirley Reine. Rams stated that the store was in the Wareham area, which Rams stated that he planned to operate as a combination video and smoke/head shop. Rams offered that he let Reine "feel him" and led Reine to believe he would do the murder, but that he never intended to do the job. Rams stated that in the months before he was arrested and given a two and half year sentence, Reine had become "amped up" about getting the job done and was "going 100 miles an hour" about having Shirley Reine killed. Rams stated that he then began to "back off" from Reine.

I informed Rams that we were interested in his direct involvement in the breaking and entering and informed him that Todd Reine and Nadia Smulliac had been indicted and arrested for the crime. I informed Rams that he had also been indicted for the same crime. Rams stated that he wanted to tell us what we were looking for. I informed Rams that we were looking for specifics in the breaking and entering case and the involvement of others in that crime. Rams then asked if this indictment would affect his release date. I advised Rams that the court would determine whether he was to be held and if so what bail would be set at. Rams stated that he already had plans to go to New Port Richey, Florida with his girlfriend. Rams asked if there was a deal on the table and what would it do to his ability to get bail or be released. Rams was advised that the issues were for the court to answer, not us. Rams stated that he couldn't say anything now, but was willing to tell us "everything" if his attorney was present.

Rams stated that he wanted us to contact his attorney and tell the attorney what "the deal" was and what information we needed and then he would be willing to sit down with us again with his attorney present.

Rams then asked what deal we could offer him. Rams was informed that we were not authorized to extend any type of deal to him and that we would contact his attorney. Rams was told that if he had information he could contact his attorney and make arrangements with his attorney to meet with us. Rams was told to consider his information as having a shelf life and not delay in contacting his attorney. Rams stated that he wanted to talk to his attorney before answering any further questions.

Rams then asked what the status of the Cartier ring which his girlfriend had turned over to police. Rams was told the ownership of the ring was still being investigated and that we could not answer any of his questions.

At that time Rams stood, went to the door and indicated to the corrections officer outside the room he was finished. The interview was then concluded.

If the state police had their way, John Rams would never set foot outside of a Massachusetts prison again. He was clearly a guy who had been given chance after chance to rehabilitate himself. Investigators are familiar with the type. The system gives them a break—even on something as brutal as carving up a guy in a gazebo in the town square—and they don't know how to move on to being just a regular person, a civilian. It's as if the criminal mind cannot be reset. John Rams was someone with a criminal mind—which is what made it so difficult for the state police to prove that what he was saying about Todd Reine wanting to whack his stepmother was actually true.

Five days before the state troopers met with Rams, Cape and Islands District Attorney Michael O'Keefe released a statement to the press regarding an arrest in a "Falmouth burglary."

Cape & Islands District Attorney Michael O'Keefe and Falmouth Chief of Police David Cusolito announced today the arrest of three individuals involved in the December, 2002, burglary of a home located at 657 East Falmouth Highway, in the Town of Falmouth:
John Rams, Jr. (DOB: 11/4/72)
  Charged with: Unarmed Burglary c. 266/15, Larceny from a Building c. 266/20 and Stealing a Will c. 266/39
Todd M. Reine (DOB: 11/10/66)
  Charged with: Unarmed Burglary c. 266/15, Stealing a Will c. 266/39 and Receiving Stolen Property c. 266/60
Nadia M. Smuliac (DOB: 8/12/82)
  Charged with: Unarmed Burglary c. 266/15 and Larceny from Building c. 266/20
John Rams, Jr. is being held at MCI Norfolk where he is currently serving a sentence. Arrangements will be made for him to appear for arraignment in Barnstable Superior Court at a later date. Todd M. Reine will be brought to Barnstable Superior Court for ar-

raignment. Nadia M. Smuliac is being held at a Connecticut facility awaiting transfer to Massachusetts for arraignment on these charges.

The charges are the result of an ongoing investigation that is being conducted by Massachusetts State Police assigned to the Cape & Islands District Attorney's office and the Falmouth Police Department. There will be no further information released at this time. Further information will be released when appropriate.

The statement made no mention of Shirley Reine's murder even if it was clear in the minds of everyone in Falmouth that cops were closing in on Todd Reine. Even Todd Reine was worried. He made a phone call to the best defense attorney in Massachusetts, Kevin Reddington.

By then, the evidence collected against Todd Reine was so damning, even Kevin Reddington could not prevent him from going to jail.

TWENTY

John Rams sat in his cell reading the letter he'd received from Nadia over and over again. Her writing was a mess, he thought. Indicative of her personality. He'd been a paranoid guy long before his arrest, and had heard stories that Todd Reine had apparently made moves on his girl. She had denied that she and Todd were romantically involved, but he had heard it from police and the street. He was heartbroken, but kept reading the letter anyway.

"Hey," Nadia wrote.

> *There is no way I can be involved in that drama with Todd. I feel used as a pawn by him. But we'll have to see.*
>
> *I'm sorry you are having bad dreams. It's most likely from all the stress and confusion around you. I'm sure there is no one you can really talk to, so all you're left with is your own thoughts.*
>
> *I believe your letters cheer me up, so I hope mine bring you some joy. Thanks to you I'm still dancing. They're not so bad up here now.*
>
> *Have you spoken to your lawyer yet, to find out the outcome on Wed.? Do you know if your case will be heard by the same judge? Lynch?*
>
> *Maybe you should write a letter to the court to see if you can take some classes on the outside for substance abuse.*

You've been and are an angel in my life and I will never forget you.
Keep your head up and hopefully I'll see you.
                                        w/love, Nadia.

The letter provided John Rams all of the ammunition he needed to make his decision on whether he should help investigators who were building a case against Todd Reine in connection with his stepmother's murder. Nadia seemed to have become one of the many women in Todd Reine's life. He followed in his father's footsteps with womanizing, just as he had in the criminal life, apparently. Rams didn't feel guilty at all that he'd told detectives about the video store that Todd Reine had promised to buy him if he shot Shirley dead. He didn't feel any sense of betrayal or guilt that he told detectives Todd Reine had said out loud in a crowd that he wanted his stepmother dead. Sure, that made him a rat. But Reine was a rat too if he slept with Nadia.

Of course, Nadia had her reasons for cheating. Rams was a violent lover for one, and she also had a drug dependency. In fact, she had aborted a child because she was afraid it would be born with drug addictions, Rams testified in court. That was the explanation he gave anyway when he was grilled by one of Todd Reine's attorneys about a brutal beating Rams had delivered to Nadia months after the burglary. He'd burned her with a cigarette, beaten her and even bitten off a piece of her lower lip.

"Do you remember what her face looked like, sir, after you dragged her by the hair and beat her?" attorney Drew Segadelli asked Rams.

"Yeah, I got a little violent," he responded. "It's not something I am proud of, Mr. Segadelli."

"The beating lasted for three days?" Segadelli asked.

"Well, she left, came back; she left and came back," Rams responded.

Rams was a believer in the old saying that what goes around, comes around. So, apparently, was Nadia.

TWENTY-ONE

In the end, John Rams will serve more time for stealing a safe for "Uncle Todd" than he did for plunging a knife into a guy twelve times, killing him. He will be in prison longer for a burglary than he was for murder. Of course, his long rap sheet didn't help matters. After his release on the murder case, Rams went to jail again, this time for assault and battery with a dangerous weapon—a conviction that only earned him 30 days in the house of correction. He would be arrested numerous times after he'd served out that sentence, for beating up a cop, distributing narcotics and breaking and entering. He was consistently given no more than a slap on the wrist, a clear signal that his cooperation with police on the Shirley Reine case was not the first time he'd traded information on a crime in exchange for a light sentence. This time, however, the judge could only be so lenient.

In September 2007, John Rams pleaded guilty to breaking into Shirley Reine's house, and received a 7- to 8-year sentence at Walpole, the prison that the Reine family believes created a version of the Falmouth Fox even more brutal than the one who'd been sentenced for that series of arsons back in 1968. After his conviction, Rams would write letters, including one to this journalist writing a book about the Falmouth Fox.

Michele, I understand that your world moves a lot faster than mine. . . . the ring was not Shirley's ring. It was in fact a 4ct emerald vintage Cartier ring. It was purchased by me *for my girl as an engagement ring. There were two people plus myself in the room when I purchased it for $1,500 along with an agreement that I would bring another $5,500 for the full payment of $7,000.*

While I was on the run from Todd and the law, I worked my underground networks. People saw my girl with the ring and the key stone cops with there too little too late investigation just assumed the ring was Shirley's. When I was finally arrested on a probation warrant I was asked all the usual questions key stone cops ask would be suspects . . .

Rams went on to ramble about a meeting he'd had with state police, a lie detector test and again, the ring.

I said, here's what I'll do. You let me call my girl and I'll get the ring. They agreed and I called my girl and told her in front of them to never let them get the ring ever. The next day I called my girl and all I could hear were metal detectors going off. She had the ring on the whole time. They coerced her into giving them the ring with a contract wich she still has. She was there when I bought the ring so she knew it wasn't Shirley's. They told my girl it was stolen from some people in Wareham or Dennis or somewhere. There was no doubt in my mind the ring was hot, but I still felt like she deserved it more than what I could give her so I tried.

My relationship with Todd and Melvin is another story. Todd was a customer at first he like women but could only get some when he was paying for it. Anyhow, I got caught up in Carver and he offered me a lawyer.

Rams claimed that the Reine boys' attorney had gotten him out of a jam.

After that I felt I owed him. That's when he said he needed a B&E done. I was never into breaking into other people's houses so I got . . . Jerome Bradley. We did it gave up the will to Todd in 2002. That's when the story begins.

John-John.

Another letter—original spelling intact—described a writing project that Rams was working on in prison.

I strongly believe everything happens for a reason. That where we are is where we're supposed to be, doing what we are supposed to be doing; seeing what we are supposed to be seeing; hearing what we are supposed to be hearing; and feeling what we are supposed to be feeling so that we know what to do next. This, I believe (what we do next) is our reason. I do not believe in coincidence. I do believe in signs and that the smaller the world we live in gets is just a sign to let us know we are on the right path. I listen to my heart and follow each path to its end.

In 2002, I found myself at the epicenter of the most insidious evil and moraly broke myself free. I almost went crazy from doing so. Then I decided that fight back against the evil, which seemed to infect everything. It infected the people around me, thier intentions, thier actions . . . thier very souls. I on the other hand, stood strong. I kept my faith in God and was able to weather everything that was thrown at me. While in the eye of the storm I had an epiphany. My soul remains uninfected and my concience remains clear.

I am stronger due to everything I have been through. Karmicly I'm good; all paid up for my actions with a little karmic credit to boot. Although my personal war against the evil that presented itself to me, I'm afraid that with all I have done to combat it, I have failed in my many attempts. I know in my heart if I could bring all of this to light, the war that I never gave up fighting could possibly be won.
                                         Sincerely, John Rams.

A P.S. included a request to send him a canteen card so he could buy soda from the vending machines.

Once a scammer, always a scammer.

Todd Reine and Nadia Smuliac would be tried together. During their seven-day trial, the two practically canoodled.

Calm and smiling as prosecutors presented the case against them, the two were clearly more than friendly.

On the seventh day, the jury came back with guilty verdicts for them both. Todd Reine actually grinned and turned around to flash his smile for the cameras covering the verdict.

Cape and Islands District Attorney Michael O'Keefe did not comment on the guilty verdicts. Instead his office wrote up a "web-only" press release as they are required to under the law.

> September 21, 2007
> Cape & Islands District Attorney Michael O'Keefe announced today that a Barnstable County Superior Court Jury convicted Todd Reine (dob: 11/10/66) and Nadia Smuliac (dob: 8/12/82) for their roles in the 2002 burglary and theft of a safe from the property of Shirley Reine at 657 East Falmouth Highway, in the Town of Falmouth. The seven day trial was prosecuted by First Assistant District Attorney Michael Trudeau.
>
> The defendants were convicted of the following offenses:
>
> Todd M. Reine: Nadia M. Smuliac:
>
> Unarmed Burglary c. 266/15 Unarmed Burglary c. 266/15
>
> Larceny of a Will c. 266/39 Larceny from Building c. 266/20
>
> A co-defendant, John Rams, Jr. pled guilty prior to trial and received a 6–7 year MCI Cedar Junction sentence for the same charges. Defendants Reine and Smuliac will be sentenced on September 28, 2007.

Again, O'Keefe made no mention of Shirley Reine's slaying in the press release. He made no mention of Charles "Jeff" Flanagan's unsolved murder; or the unexplained disappearances of Wanda Reine and Paul Alwardt. O'Keefe did not attend the sentencing for Reine and Smuliac either. It would just be another place where reporters could fire questions at him that he would not answer, questions like: "Will anyone ever be held accountable for the murder of Shirley Reine?"

On September 28, Todd Reine was led shackled into the Barnstable Criminal Court to face Judge Gary Nickerson.

"There is an element of cold-heartedness to this crime," Nickerson told Reine. He then sentenced the now 40-year-old Reine to 4 to 5 years at Walpole, the prison where his father had served less than 2 years, 35 years earlier, when Todd was a toddler himself. His attorney Kevin Reddington immediately bellowed that the sentence was not fair—Reine did not have a criminal history and was a devoted father to his four children (even if he did have a history of not paying child support for them). Nickerson was unmoved. Reddington remains convinced that Todd Reine is being held not because he was found guilty of orchestrating the robbery at his stepmother's house, but because he is a suspect in Shirley Reine's murder. The sentence of 4 to 5 years in prison when he didn't even enter the house was unheard of, Reddington said, especially considering that Todd Reine had never been convicted of any other crimes.

"It was a very stiff sentence, and it was payback," Reddington said. "Right now he's been classified as a minimum prisoner. Someone put their finger on the scale and prevented him from being transferred to a minimum security prison. I don't want to say who put their finger on the scale, but let's say that this case has political motivations.

"Todd's the type of guy who gets along with everyone. The inmates like him. The guards like him. So he'll be okay in a maximum security facility. But it's not right. The only reason he is there is because he is an object of interest in an open homicide investigation," Reddington said. "An open homicide investigation that is going nowhere."

Judge Nickerson did not cut Smuliac any slack either. In fact, Nickerson was not known for cutting anyone any slack. He had been praised by domestic violence advocates that same year after he'd delivered a strange sentencing memorandum to a convicted rapist and batterer who'd pleaded guilty to breaking into an ex-girlfriend's house where he raped and beat her: that if he ever wanted to move in with a woman again upon his release from prison, he would have to tell the new love exactly how violent he had been with other women. The move was hailed across the state.

Smuliac was sentenced to 2 years at the Barnstable House of Correction. Nickerson told her attorneys after they pleaded for leniency: "She knew exactly what she was doing. Any suggestion that she was just dragged along falls on deaf ears today."

Both Reine and Smuliac are currently appealing their convictions. It was no secret that Todd Reine was the prime suspect in the Shirley Reine homicide, and prosecutors were hoping that the heavy sentence would provoke him into confessing. The last thing anyone in Falmouth wanted to see was Todd Reine get away with the same types of crimes his father was allegedly able to pull off under the nose of a police department now tainted by the actions of a handful of accused dirty cops. Especially the crusaders, the police officers like Kris Bohnenberger and Rick Smith, who were irate that Melvin Reine was able to rule Falmouth like he did without any justice for his victims.

As of this writing, it looked as if the Shirley Reine murder investigation would net the same result as the probing of Wanda Reine's disappearance, the Paul Alwardt homicide and the slaying of Charles Flanagan: none.

The gilded fox on top of Melvin Reine's house remains a taunt to the town. A reputed lifetime of crime landed Reine in prison for less than two years total. He did outfox Falmouth in the end. And many fear that his son Todd Reine will be able to pull off the same shady maneuvers he learned from his dad.

TWENTY-TWO

Melvin Reine Sr. continues to spend his days at the Taunton State Hospital in a locked ward for the criminally insane. A week after his wife was found dead by an assassin's bullets, a psychologist was asked to write up a report for the Cape Cod Probate and Family Courts. After all, someone had to see after Melvin Reine Sr. now that Shirley was dead. It certainly would not be Todd.

In the days after his brother was charged with the burglary at Shirley Reine's house—a robbery which investigators believe he had nothing to do with—Melvin Jr. busied himself working a trash route for a garbage hauler not affiliated with Five Star Enterprises. He had a tidy house in Falmouth, a wife and a couple of kids. He was staying out of trouble and wanted to stay out of the public spotlight. He refused several requests for interviews, and would not answer the door to his business, Reine Construction. He did not make the long trip to Taunton State Hospital to visit his father. What purpose would that serve? He had no interest in watching his father drool.

It was over as far as Melvin Reine Jr. was concerned. He did not want anything to do with the lawsuit anymore. He did not want anything to do with the Reine compound or the people who lived on it. He wanted nothing to do with his father or with Shirley's sister Loretta Gilfoy, who was now in charge of her sister's estate—meaning she was also in charge of Melvin Reine's money.

Five Star Enterprises had been sold to a family friend,

John Boyle—the man who said that Shirley Reine "was no Cinderella."

The hospital needed to find a new guardian for Melvin Reine, and wrote up a report to alert the court how quickly that issue needed to be expedited. On May 17, 2005, Dr. Muhammed Absar wrote:

> This is a 64-year-old right handed Cape Verdean male who was admitted to Taunton State Hospital on 11/29/01 for a 15B commitment for the evaluation of competency with charges of threat to commit a crime, assault by dangerous weapon and destruction of property. Pt has no prior psychiatric history apart from a work-up for dementia at Falmouth Hospital few weeks prior to his admission to TSH. He has had multiple extensive Neuropsychiatric work up done since his admission to TSH . . . he was clinically diagnosed with Fronto-Temporal Dementia Syndrome (Pick's Disease). Since his admission to TSH, Pt has progressively declined in his activities of daily livings and functioning and currently showing evidence of Advanced Fronto-Temporal Dementia (Pick's Disease) with multiple, severe mood swings . . . He has bizarre rituals including urinating in his room and in other patient's beds, delusions and hallucinations. He is mute, not interacting with staff and not making eye contact. He is unpredictable and at high risk for injury to himself and others and needs total nursing care and constant assistance and redirection. His mental status over the past year showing evidence of rapid decline in memory, intellectual functions, increasingly bizarre and disorganized behavior (urinating in his room, refusing to shower, self care, meals) obsessive-compulsive disorders (including hoarding behavior, inflexibility, compulsions), delusions and impulsivity. His dementia is progressively worsening. He is on a DNR (Do Not Resuscitate).

Patient's power of attorney was his wife Shirley

Reine who had been actively involved with all of his care. Unfortunately she was murdered last week.

Treatment team hereby request the court for an appointment of a new guardian as soon as possible to continue his medical /psychiatric care as he lacks the capacity to make any informed decisions for all.

The Falmouth Fox had bragged way back in 2001 when he was arrested for threatening to blow the tourist's head off that he would never face a trial. He was aware that the feds wanted to charge him with using his land on Old Barnstable Road as an illegal dump. He knew that his sons had sung to the police and that his brother had fingered him in John Busby's shooting. But if he was crazy, no one could charge him with anything. He knew it. His attorney Rick Mycock knew it. And both of those men were right.

The Falmouth Fox had won again—depending on how one looked at it.

Sure, he was in a locked ward with no way out. But it wasn't Walpole. Melvin Reine was not imprisoned with bars and surly correction officers.

Judging from the doctor's report, Melvin Reine's own mind was his prison. He was alone in the hospital and it was very likely that he would die there. Alone.

TWENTY-THREE

Todd was in jail. Melvin Jr. was lying low. And Shirley Reine's will was very specific. Everything that was left to her by Melvin would be left to her sister Loretta Gilfoy. Her sister had already inherited Shirley's beloved dogs, and her pet goat Ricky had since been sent to live on a sprawling Cape Cod farm. Loretta had also grown close to Michael Domingues, Shirley's lover, the man who found her body that terrible morning in May 2005. They had become unified in their mission to find the killer who'd cut down Shirley Reine, and that common goal had brought them close together. Today, Loretta looks back on Shirley's life and can understand why men like Michael Domingues had found her sister so irresistible.

There was really only one man who made Shirley's heart flutter in that same way though: the Falmouth Fox.

"My sister was hot to trot, she was gorgeous. She had a nice little body, and long brown hair and wore her little miniskirts. It would not be a surprise that men would be attracted to her. Not at all. But she was in love with Melvin. My father didn't like it. No one liked it. He was the Falmouth Fox. But Shirley couldn't be talked out of it, she loved him," Gilfoy remembered. Gilfoy had been at her sister's side since the time the Reine boys were young.

To this day she does not want to believe that they could be behind Shirley Reine's murder. "Melvin has kids all over the place. Shirley did treat Todd's children, her step-grandchildren, like they were her own. She loved Melly and

Todd very much. They spent most of their time growing up with her anyway," she remembered. She talked to both of them after Shirley Reine was murdered, and they said they just wanted to clear their names in the murder. "I told them, 'What do you expect people to think?' Here it was, a week before the trial, and Shirley ends up dead. Of course it's the talk of the town that the boys did it. Of course people are going to say that they did it."

Like most residents in Falmouth, she wishes that someone would be charged with the homicide. It would settle a lot of resentment among people who still blame the ineptitude of the old Falmouth police force and the clenched eyes of town selectmen who allowed Melvin Reine to run amok. "The Falmouth Police Department is so corrupted. I hope they all get investigated. They have not been very kind to me since Shirley was killed."

She blames the Falmouth town officials for her sister's murder, for the unexplained disappearances of people close to the Falmouth Fox and for the slaying of Shirley's teen-aged boyfriend. She'd like to think that John Rams was the killer, and that he'd murdered her sister of his own accord without any input from the Reine brothers. She will never be entirely sure, though.

"I've never heard of John Rams, I don't know about him. But, he's a drug addict. He's already killed someone before. I just don't know. I know Melvin and Todd did not actually do it," Loretta mused. "Did they have someone do it? . . . I don't want to comment on that."

She still finds herself pulled back to that garage where she saw her sister's blood-splattered body so many years ago. To this day, however, Loretta Gilfoy has not put in a claim for her sister's house or for any earnings from the lucrative estate that she automatically inherited when Shirley Reine was murdered. She can't bring herself to do it.

"I saw her in the garage the next morning. That yellow shirt, all stained with blood, sticks in my mind. I literally shook remembering seeing her just lying there up against the door. I'm just praying to God that she went instantly, and

I hope to God she didn't see who did it, that she didn't suffer that feeling of fear looking at her killer. And I'm sorry that she had to lie there all night. I feel like the Reines can rot there. I don't want anything from them. My sister was murdered for that property. I don't want anything to do with it.

"It's evil land and I don't want to set foot on it."

TWENTY-FOUR

Detective Captain Roman "Skip" Medeiros remains a supervisor on the Falmouth police force. He testified on his nephew Todd's behalf at his trial and still remains close to Melvin Jr. Ask him about his missing sister Wanda and anger creases his eyebrows. Not that his sister is still unaccounted for, but that someone asked about it.

"I am a professional police officer and I have been for thirty-one years," he said in his office at Falmouth police headquarters. Looking around, one can't help but wonder if Melvin Reine had been in that very room at one time, sitting in that very chair. Maybe he had been there many times. It was the office of a Falmouth police supervisor, and the Falmouth police commanders had been known to pull strings on behalf of Melvin Reine over the years.

"My personal relationship to this case has nothing to do with the investigation at all. My family's involvement . . . it's still painful every time this stuff comes up in the press about the Reine family," Medeiros said. "This case remains a joint investigation."

Of course state police homicide investigators questioned Medeiros about where he was the night Shirley Reine was murdered. He provided an alibi. Even John Busby was questioned in the case. After all, he had motive. Shirley Reine was in the station wagon the night that her husband squeezed those shotgun blasts off so long ago, her brother-in-law claimed. Now she was dead. It was not that far of a stretch to think that Busby had acted out the revenge that he had fantasized about for decades. After a brief grilling, Busby was cleared. He was nowhere near Cape Cod when Shirley Reine was shot dead. And she was not the shooter anyway. Just a witness. Culpable, yes. Worth killing, no.

Nonetheless, everyone close to the Shirley Reine murder case thought it best that the highest-ranking detective in the Falmouth Police Department remove himself from the case entirely. Medeiros is not directly involved in the Shirley Reine homicide investigation.

Cape and Islands District Attorney Michael O'Keefe is still not talking—not in a towel or otherwise. Recently he sat in his office in Hyannis and puffed on a cigarette. An ashtray on his desk overflowed with menthol butts. He has steadfastly refused to comment on the pace of the investigation into Shirley Reine's murder.

"Shirley Reine was the victim of a homicide. The matter is under investigation. We spend our time working these cases, not talking about them," O'Keefe said. "That's how we are successful at resolving these cases."

John Busby's fight to extend the statute of limitations is still stalled on Boston's Beacon Hill. John Reine's confession meant nothing in the end. Busby and his family returned to their beloved Cape Cod in the summer of 2008. John Busby and his daughter Cylin spent months on a book and publicity tour to promote their memoir. They were also interviewed by the TV show *48 Hours*, along with retired Falmouth Police Officer Rick Smith and State Trooper Kris Bohnenberger.

The town of Falmouth pays Busby a paltry pension, which he supplements by working at his local Home Depot. It is clear that no one will ever be charged with the attempt on his life that left him unable to eat or speak properly ever again. At the very least Busby should be collecting a full disability retirement pension, but Falmouth town selectmen—among whom is Ahmed Mustafa, the cop who'd sold Melvin Reine the station wagon used in the attempt on Busby's life—have voted no on that move. Mustafa also declined to be interviewed.

The crusaders in the Falmouth police force who were

dedicated to rooting out the corruption that allowed a guy like Melvin Reine to create a criminal enterprise in a small New England town continue to do the work of the Lord; battling back against the malignant politicians who are afraid to look at how the department was able to hide the actions of the Falmouth Fox for such a staggeringly long time.

To this day, Loretta Gilfoy still likes to remind anyone who will listen that her lifelong hometown is "not the sweet little oasis everyone thinks it is."